Flash MX: Basic

Student Manual

THOMSON

COURSE TECHNOLOGY

Australia • Canada • Mexico • Singapore
Spain • United Kingdom • United States

Flash MX: Basic

VP and GM of Courseware:	Michael Springer
Series Product Managers:	Caryl Bahner-Guhin and Adam A. Wilcox
Developmental Editor:	Jim O'Shea
Project Editor:	Don Tremblay
Key Tester:	Bill Bateman
Series Designer:	Adam A. Wilcox
Cover Designer:	Steve Deschene

For more information contact:

Course Technology
25 Thomson Place
Boston, MA 02210

Or find us on the Web at: www.course.com

For permission to use material from this text or product, contact us by

• Web: www.thomsonrights.com
• Phone: 1-800-730-2214
• Fax: 1-800-730-2215

Trademarks

Course ILT is a trademark of Course Technology.

Some of the product names and company names used in this book have been used for identification purposes only and may be trademarks or registered trademarks of their respective manufacturers and sellers.

Disclaimer

Course Technology reserves the right to revise this publication and make changes from time to time in its content without notice.

ISBN 0-619-07474-4

Printed in the United States of America

3 4 5 6 7 8 9 PM 08 07 06

Contents

Flash MX: Basic

Introduction

After reading this introduction, you will know how to:

A Use Course Technology ILT manuals in general.

B Use prerequisites, a target student description, course objectives, and a skills inventory to properly set your expectations for the course.

C Re-key this course after class.

Topic A: About the manual

Course Technology ILT philosophy

Course Technology ILT manuals facilitate your learning by providing structured interaction with the software itself. While we provide text to explain difficult concepts, the hands-on activities are the focus of our courses. By paying close attention as your instructor leads you through these activities, you will learn the skills and concepts effectively.

We believe strongly in the instructor-led classroom. During class, focus on your instructor. Our manuals are designed and written to facilitate your interaction with your instructor, and not to call attention to manuals themselves.

We believe in the basic approach of setting expectations, delivering instruction, and providing summary and review afterwards. For this reason, lessons begin with objectives and end with summaries. We also provide overall course objectives and a course summary to provide both an introduction to and closure on the entire course.

Manual components

The manuals contain these major components:

- Table of contents
- Introduction
- Units
- Course summary
- Quick reference
- Index

Each element is described below.

Table of contents

The table of contents acts as a learning roadmap.

Introduction

The introduction contains information about our training philosophy and our manual components, features, and conventions. It contains target student, prerequisite, objective, and setup information for the specific course.

Units

Units are the largest structural component of the course content. A unit begins with a title page that lists objectives for each major subdivision, or topic, within the unit. Within each topic, conceptual and explanatory information alternates with hands-on activities. Units conclude with a summary comprising one paragraph for each topic, and an independent practice activity that gives you an opportunity to practice the skills you've learned.

The conceptual information takes the form of text paragraphs, exhibits, lists, and tables. The activities are structured in two columns, one telling you what to do, the other providing explanations, descriptions, and graphics.

Course summary

This section provides a text summary of the entire course. It is useful for providing closure at the end of the course. The course summary also indicates the next course in this series, if there is one, and lists additional resources you might find useful as you continue to learn about the software.

Quick reference

The quick reference is an at-a-glance job aid summarizing some of the more common features of the software.

Index

The index at the end of this manual makes it easy for you to find information about a particular software component, feature, or concept.

Manual conventions

We've tried to keep the number of elements and the types of formatting to a minimum in the manuals. This aids in clarity and makes the manuals more classically elegant looking. But there are some conventions and icons you should know about.

Convention/Icon	Description
Italic text	In conceptual text, indicates a new term or feature.
Bold text	In unit summaries, indicates a key term or concept. In an independent practice activity, indicates an explicit item that you select, choose, or type.
`Code font`	Indicates code or syntax.
`Longer strings of ▶` `code will look ▶` `like this.`	In the hands-on activities, any code that's too long to fit on a single line is divided into segments by one or more continuation characters (▶). This code should be entered as a continuous string of text.
Select **bold item**	In the left column of hands-on activities, bold sans-serif text indicates an explicit item that you select, choose, or type.
Keycaps like (↵ ENTER)	Indicate a key on the keyboard you must press.

Hands-on activities

The hands-on activities are the most important parts of our manuals. They are divided into two primary columns. The "Here's how" column gives short instructions to you about what to do. The "Here's why" column provides explanations, graphics, and clarifications. Here's a sample:

Do it!

A-1:   Creating a commission formula

Here's how	Here's why
1 Open Sales	This is an oversimplified sales compensation worksheet. It shows sales totals, commissions, and incentives for five sales reps.
2 Observe the contents of cell F4		F4 ▼	=	=E4*C_Rate	 The commission rate formulas use the name "C_Rate" instead of a value for the commission rate.

For these activities, we have provided a collection of data files designed to help you learn each skill in a real-world business context. As you work through the activities, you will modify and update these files. Of course, you might make a mistake and, therefore, want to re-key the activity starting from scratch. To make it easy to start over, you will rename each data file at the end of the first activity in which the file is modified. Our convention for renaming files is to add the word "My" to the beginning of the file name. In the above activity, for example, a file called "Sales" is being used for the first time. At the end of this activity, you would save the file as "My sales," thus leaving the "Sales" file unchanged. If you make a mistake, you can start over using the original "Sales" file.

In some activities, however, it may not be practical to rename the data file. If you want to retry one of these activities, ask your instructor for a fresh copy of the original data file.

Topic B: Setting your expectations

Properly setting your expectations is essential to your success. This topic will help you do that by providing:

- Prerequisites for this course
- A description of the target student at whom the course is aimed
- A list of the objectives for the course
- A skills assessment for the course

Course prerequisites

Before taking this course, you should be familiar with personal computers and the use of a keyboard and a mouse. Furthermore, this course assumes that you've completed the following courses or have equivalent experience:

- *Microsoft Windows 98: Basic* or *Microsoft Windows 2000: Basic*

Target student

This course is designed for those who have a good idea how to create visually appealing shapes and diagrams as well as some basic graphic design skills. You will get the most out of this course if you are familiar with Web browsers, Internet and graphic design terminologies, and if your goal is to design animation for the Web.

Course objectives

These overall course objectives will give you an idea about what to expect from the course. It is also possible that they will help you see that this course is not the right one for you. If you think you either lack the prerequisite knowledge or already know most of the subject matter to be covered, you should let your instructor know that you think you are misplaced in the class.

After completing this course, you will know how to:

- Explore Flash MX, use the Help feature, and open an existing document.
- Create, select, edit, and handle shapes by using the various tools.
- Apply colors to shapes, and create custom colors, gradients, and line styles.
- Combine and group shapes, import bitmaps, and convert them to vector shapes.
- Add text to a document and format the text.
- Use layers to arrange shapes in a document and modify the layers.
- Play an animation, create a frame-by-frame animation use Onion Skin, and work with templates.

Skills inventory

Use the following form to gauge your skill level entering the class. For each skill listed, rate your familiarity from 1 to 5, with five being the most familiar. *This is not a test.* Rather, it is intended to provide you with an idea of where you're starting from at the beginning of class. If you're wholly unfamiliar with all the skills, you might not be ready for the class. If you think you already understand all of the skills, you might need to move on to the next course in the series. In either case, you should let your instructor know as soon as possible.

Skill	1	2	3	4	5
Start Flash, open an existing file, and explore the Toolbox and panels					
Get help by using the Contents, Index, and Search tabs					
Close files and exit Flash					
Create shapes by using the Line, Rectangle, Oval, Pen, and Pencil Tool					
Select shapes by using the Arrow Tool and the Lasso Tool					
Edit shapes by using the Arrow Tool and the Eraser Tool					
View, move, copy, and delete shapes					
Apply stroke and fill colors to a shape by using the Paint Bucket, Ink Bottle, and Eye dropper tools					
Create custom colors, gradients, and line styles					
Combine and group shapes					
Import raster images and convert them to vector images					
Use the Text Tool to create an extending, fixed, and a scrollable text block					
Format text by changing the font, font size, color, font style, text alignment, skewing and scaling, and by converting to shapes					
Create, rearrange, and delete layers					
Rename, lock, and hide layers					
Use the Timeline, create a frame-by-frame animation, and use onion skin to modify the contents of frames					
Work with templates					

Topic C: Re-keying the course

If you have the proper hardware and software, you can re-key this course after class. This section explains what you'll need in order to do so, and how to do it.

Computer requirements

To re-key this course, your personal computer must have:

- A keyboard and a mouse
- A Pentium processor with minimum 200 MHz
- A minimum of 64 MB RAM (128 MB RAM recommended)
- A minimum of 85 MB hard disk space
- A CD-ROM drive
- An SVGA monitor at 800×600 resolution
- Internet access is required if you will be downloading data files from www.courseilt.com

Setup instructions to re-key the course

Before you re-key the course, you will need to perform the following steps.

1 Install Windows 2000 Professional according to the software manufacturer's instructions. Select the typical installation with all the default settings. You can also use Windows 98, Windows Me, Windows NT 4 (with Service Pack 5), Windows XP Home, or Windows XP Pro. The screen shots in this course were taken using Windows 2000, so your screen might look different on a different operating system.

2 Install Flash MX according to the software manufacturer's instructions. A typical installation is required.

3 Download the Student Data examples for the course. You can download the student data directly to your machines, to a central location on your own network, or to a disk.

 a Connect to www.courseilt.com/instructor_tools.html.

 b Click the link for Macromedia Flash to display a page of course listings, and then click the link for Flash MX: Basic.

 c Click the link for downloading the data disk files, and follow the instructions that appear on your screen.

Unit 1

Getting started with Flash MX

Unit time: 50 minutes

Complete this unit, and you'll know how to:

A Start Flash, open an existing file, and explore the Toolbox and panels.

B Get Help by using the Contents, Index, and Search tabs.

C Close file and exit Flash.

Topic A: Introducing Flash

Explanation

Flash MX is a graphics package that you can use to add animations to Web pages. You can also use Flash to create navigation controls and animated sequences with sound.

Starting Flash

To start Flash, choose Start, Programs, Macromedia, Macromedia Flash MX.

Components of a Flash window

In addition to the components found in other Windows applications, a Flash window includes the Toolbox, the Stage, the Workspace, the Timeline window, and the various panels.

The following table describes the components of the Flash window:

Component	Description
Toolbox	Contains several button-like tools that you can use for drawing, selecting, editing, coloring, and viewing images.
Menu bar	Contains menus that you can use to interact with Flash. Each menu has a set of commands that help you perform various functions, such as opening a file, creating a new file, editing images, and creating animations.
Timeline	Is used to control the behavior of shapes and images in a file and to arrange them according to the sequence of the document. A *file* is called a document in Flash. The Timeline consists of various components, such as layers, frames, and playhead. It also includes folders to organize layers.
Title bar	Displays the name of the application and the current document.
Panels	Helps you to monitor, arrange, and modify the images in the document. You can view or hide the panels by using the Window menu option.
Workspace	Is the gray area that surrounds the Stage. You can use this area to place images that you do not want to be printed.
Stage	Is the white rectangular area where you can create and view the various components of a document.
Zoom box	Displays the current magnification of the image relative to its actual size. You can change the magnification of the image by either selecting a magnification level from the Zoom list or entering a value in the Zoom box. By default, it contains the value 49%.

Toolbox   Menu bar   Timeline   Zoom box   Title bar

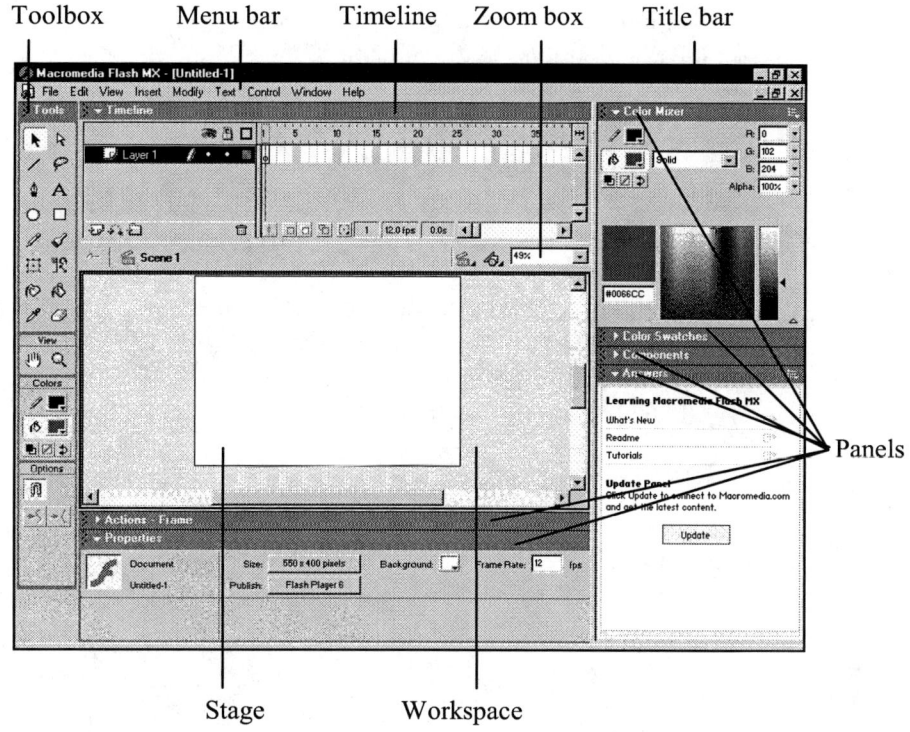

Exhibit 1-1: A sample Flash window

Stage   Workspace

Do it!

A-1:   Starting Flash and examining the Flash interface

Here's how	Here's why
1 Choose **Start**, **Programs**, **Macromedia**, **Macromedia Flash MX**	To start Flash MX. You'll learn about the Flash interface.
2 Observe the screen	You see a window with a title bar, menu bar, Toolbox, panels, the stage, the workspace, and the Timeline, as shown in Exhibit 1-1.
3 Observe the menu bar	In addition to the menus commonly available in other Windows applications, there are three menus unique to Flash. They are Modify, Text, and Control.
4 Observe the Toolbox	You can see the different types of tools, such as Lasso, Pen, Rectangle, Free Transform, and Zoom.
5 Observe the panels	There are various panels in Flash. The six active panels in the window are Color Mixer, Answers, Color Swatches, Components, Actions - Frame, and Properties.

Opening an existing file

Explanation

To open a file, choose File, Open. The Open dialog box appears. From the Look in list, select the folder and the file you want to open, and click Open.

Do it!

A-2:   Opening a file

Here's how	Here's why
1 Choose **File, Open...**	The Open dialog box appears.
2 From the Look in list, select **Student Data**	
Navigate to the current unit folder	
3 Select **Home page**	This file contains the Outlander Spices Home page that you'll work on.
4 Click **Open**	The Outlander Spices Home page appears on the stage. A file in Flash is called a document.
5 Click the Zoom box, as shown
(The Zoom box is at the upper right corner of the Flash window.) A pop-up list appears. It contains magnification levels for viewing documents.
6 From the list, select **50%**	To reduce the size of the movie to 50% of its original size, so that you are able to see the entire Web page.

The Toolbox

Explanation

The Toolbox is divided into four sections:

- **Tools** — Contains tools for selecting, drawing, and editing shapes or images.
- **View** — Contains tools that help you see an image in different modes.
- **Colors** — Contains colors that are currently used in a shape.
- **Options** — Contains modifiers for the various tools. The modifiers appear only when a tool is selected in the Tools section.

The following table describes the functions of some of the tools on the Toolbox:

Tool	Tool name	Description
	Arrow Tool	Select, move, or resize an object.
	Rectangle Tool	Create rectangles and squares.
	Text Tool	Insert text blocks.
	Pencil Tool	Draw freeform lines and shapes.
	Paint Bucket Tool	Change the fill color of shapes. *Fill* defines the color that you will paint the inside of an object with.
	Eraser Tool	Erase unwanted parts of a shape.
	Zoom Tool	View a shape magnified.
	Free Transform Tool	Transform images, instances, or text blocks. You can resize, rotate, distort, or envelop images, instances, or text blocks.

Panels

You use panels to modify the characteristics of images, such as changing the height and width, selecting colors, and changing text settings. In addition, you can also move, group or separate the panels themselves by dragging the tab that contains the panel name.

If you need more space in your window while working, you can hide a panel. To do so, double-click the title bar and the panel will minimize or maximize. To close a panel, Right click it and choose Close Panel.

After you get comfortable with Flash, you might find that you use some panels frequently. You can then close the panels you don't use, align your favorite panels, and then save the panel set by choosing Window, Save Panel Layout. You can open your panel set by choosing Window, Panel Set and then name you gave it.

The following table describes some of the default panels:

Panel	Name	Description
	Color Mixer	Used to create and edit solid colors and gradient fills, and create new colors or adjust the alpha of the existing colors. The *alpha* for a color determines its level of transparency.
	Properties	Used for customizing the workspace. You can change font properties, move objects, add sound, and set and view information about instances. It is also known as the *Property Inspector*.
	Answers	Used to get help on using Flash, information about the new features, and tips from the Macromedia Web site.
	Components	Used to create reusable drag and drop components. It has seven pre-built components: CheckBox, ComboBox, ListBox, PushButton, RadioButton, ScrollBar, and ScrollPane.

Do it!   **A-3:** **Discussing tools and panels**

Questions and answers

1 What are the different sections of the Toolbox?

2 Where will you create a new fill color?

3 Where will you change the font size and color of a text?

4 Where will you find the option to Update Flash MX?

5 Where will you add user-defined components?

Topic B: Getting Help

Explanation

You can use Flash Help to get information on topics you have never worked on or need more details about. For example, before you work with Flash MX, you can become familiar with its interface by referring to Help. You access Help from the Help menu of the Flash window. You can also use Help Lessons and the Answers Panel to access tutorials on Flash.

The Using Flash option

To open Help, choose Help, Using Flash. The Flash Help page opens. The page is divided into two panes, as shown in Exhibit 1-2. The left pane is divided into two parts. The upper part contains a link to the Macromedia Web site. The lower part contains three tabs: Contents, Index, and Search. By default, the Contents tab is active.

The right pane displays information related to a topic selected in the left pane. However, when you open the Help page, it contains the logo for Macromedia Flash MX as shown in Exhibit 1-2.

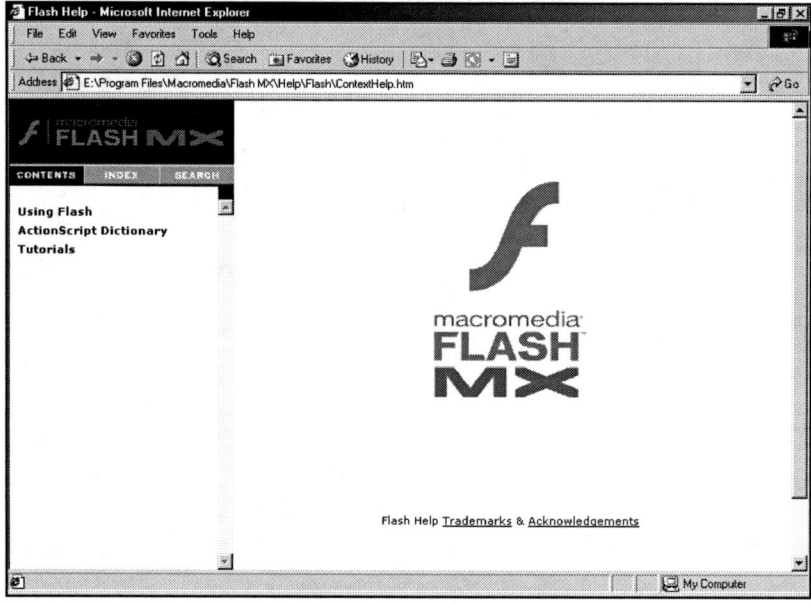

Exhibit 1-2: The Flash Help window

You can use the three Help tabs as follows:

- The *Contents* tab provides you with a list of available Help categories. You use this tab to scroll through the Help categories.
- The *Index* tab provides an alphabetical list of all the available Help topics, like the index of a book.
- The *Search* tab is used to search the entire Help file for a keyword or phrase that you type. It displays a list of all the help topics that include at least one occurrence of the keyword or phrase.

Do it!

B-1: Opening the Help page

Here's how	Here's why
1 Choose **Help, Using Flash**	To open the Flash Help page.
2 Observe the html page	The page is divided into two panes, the left pane and the right pane, as shown in Exhibit 1-2.
Observe the left pane	The left pane is divided into two parts. The upper part contains a link to the Macromedia Web site. The lower part contains three tabs: Contents, Index, and Search. By default, the Contents tab is active.
Observe the right pane	The right pane displays information related to a selected topic. When you first open the Help page, it shows the Macromedia Flash MX logo.

The Contents tab

Explanation

The Contents tab shows a list of Help categories available. Some category names appear in bold. These contain multiple subtopics. To display the list of subtopics under a category, click the category name. The color of the selected text changes to purple and a list of the subtopics appears under the selected category.

To display the contents of a subtopic, click the subtopic. The contents appear on the right pane of the page.

Do it!

B-2: Using the Contents tab

Here's how	Here's why
1 Observe the left pane	The Contents tab provides a hierarchical list of the available Help topics.
2 Click **Using Flash**	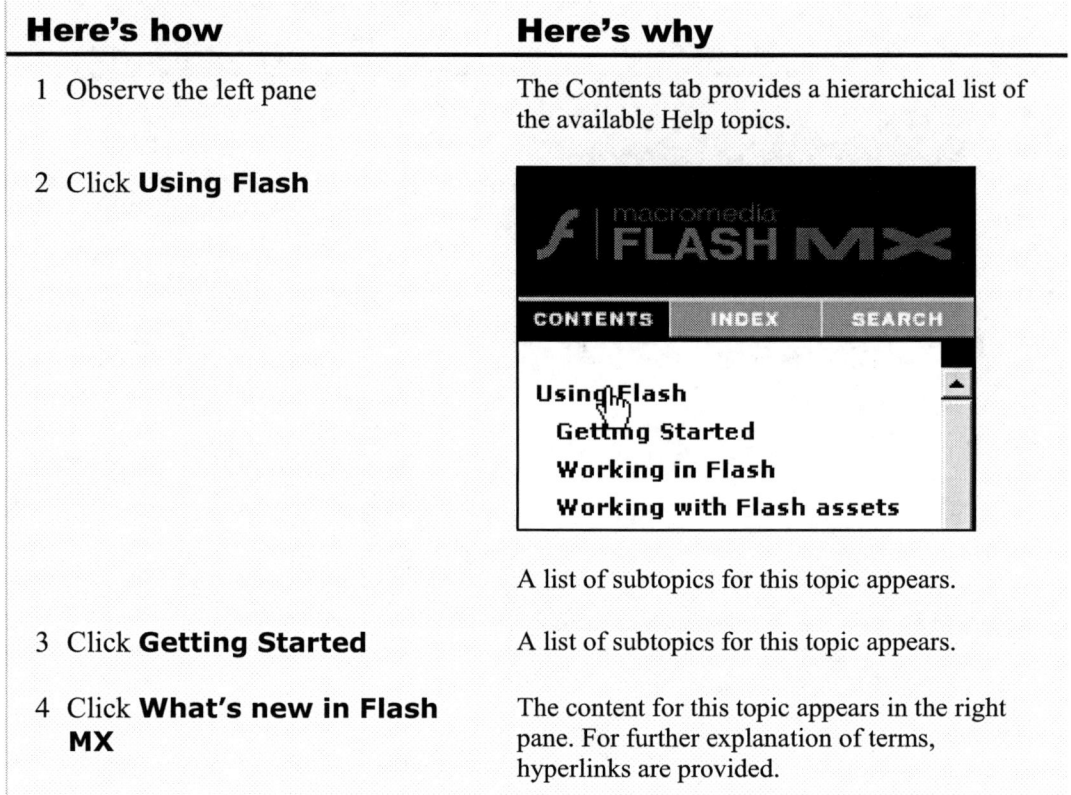
	A list of subtopics for this topic appears.
3 Click **Getting Started**	A list of subtopics for this topic appears.
4 Click **What's new in Flash MX**	The content for this topic appears in the right pane. For further explanation of terms, hyperlinks are provided.

The Index tab

Explanation

The Index tab contains an alphabetical list. You can look for information by first clicking one of the letters, which displays a list of the topics starting with that letter. You can then scroll down the list to find the topic you need. For example, you can search for information related to shapes by clicking the letter "S" and then looking for the topic related to shapes in the list that appears.

Do it!

B-3: Using the Index tab

Here's how	Here's why
1 Click the **Index** tab	
	An alphabetical list appears. You can search for a topic by clicking one of the letters.
2 Click **P**	(A list of the topics starting with the letter P appears.) You'll use the Index feature to get information about the Pen Tool.
3 Scroll down the list to locate the text, Pen Tool	
4 Click **Pen tool**	To display information about the Pen Tool.

The Search tab

Explanation

By using the Search tab you can search for specific word(s) in the Help topics, instead of searching for information by category. Help displays a list of all the topics that contain the word(s) that you specify and also the number of such topics. The Search feature is similar to the Index feature, with two key differences:

- The Search feature scans the entire text of all the Help documents for the keyword you entered. It then displays a list of all the documents that contain at least one occurrence of that keyword. This is a more detailed search than the Index feature.

- When you type a word, the second list displays related keywords to narrow down the search. If you select a keyword from the second list, the right panel of the Help page displays a topic containing the keyword (as shown in Exhibit 1-3). This can reduce the search time.

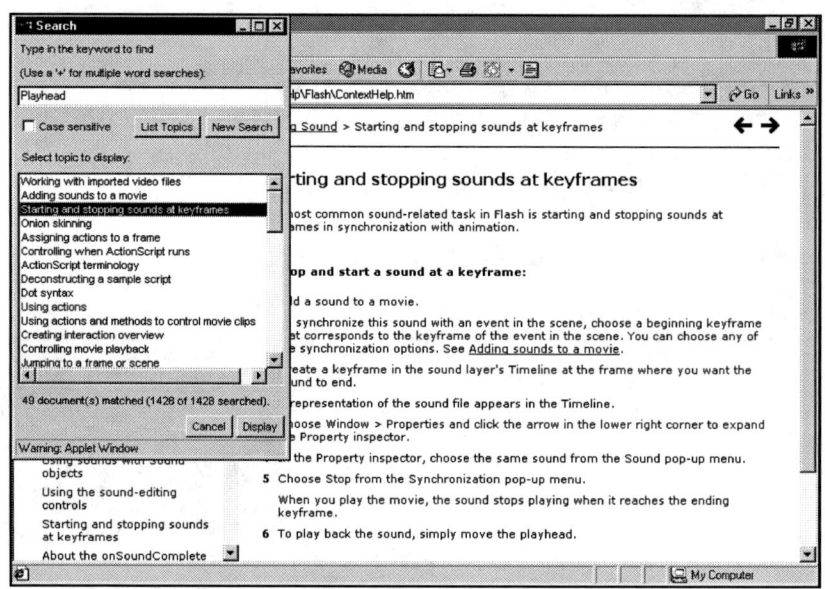

Exhibit 1-3: The Search window in the Help page

Do it!

B-4: Using the Search tab

Here's how	Here's why
1 Activate the Search tab	To open the Search window.
2 In the box, type **Playhead**	As shown in Exhibit 1-3.
3 Click **List Topics**	There are 49 topics containing the word Playhead.
4 From the list, select **Moving the playhead**	(Scroll down.) You'll view help about this topic.
5 Click **Display**	The related information appears in the right pane of the Flash Help page.
6 Close the Search window	
7 Close the Flash Help page	

Topic C: Closing files and exiting Flash

Explanation

To close a document in Flash, choose File, Close. You can also click the Close button on the upper-right corner of the window's title bar.

To exit Flash, choose File, Exit. You can also click the Close button on the upper-right corner of the Flash window's title bar.

Do it!

C-1:   Closing a file and exiting Flash

Here's how	Here's why
1 Choose **File, Close**	To close the open file.
2 Choose **File, Exit**	To close Flash.

Unit summary: Getting started with Flash MX

Topic A   In this unit, you learned how to **start Flash** and **open a file**. You examined the various **components of the Flash window**, including **Toolbox** and **panels**.

Topic B   Next, you learned how to use the **Flash Help** feature, including the **Contents tab**, **Index tab**, and **Search tab**.

Topic C   Finally, you learned how to **close** a file and **exit** Flash.

Independent practice activity

1 Start Macromedia Flash MX.

2 Open **Practice page**.

3 Using the Search tab, find help on **The Brush Tool**.

4 Close the Search window.

5 Using the Index tab get help on **shapes**.

6 Close the Flash Help page.

7 Close Practice page.

8 Close Flash.

U n i t   2

Creating shapes

Unit time: 60 minutes

Complete this unit, and you'll know how to:

A Create shapes by using the Line, Rectangle, Oval, Pen, and Pencil Tool.

B Select shapes by using the Arrow Tool and the Lasso Tool.

C Edit shapes by using the Arrow Tool and the Eraser Tool.

D View, move, copy, and delete shapes.

Topic A: Creating basic shapes

Explanation You can create basic shapes such as lines, rectangles, or ovals by using the corresponding shape tool.

The Line Tool

You use the Line Tool to draw straight lines. To draw a line:

1 Select the Line Tool from the Toolbox.

2 Place the pointer at a position where you want the line to start on the Stage. The pointer changes to a plus sign.

3 Drag the pointer to draw a line of the length you need and then release the mouse.

Rulers

Rulers help you locate and position shapes on the Stage. Rulers appear along the top and left side of the work area. By default, the origin of the ruler is at the upper left corner of the Stage. To view the rulers, choose View, Rulers.

Rulers track the pointer's position on the Stage. By default, divisions on the rulers are in pixels. You can change the measurement units to millimeters, centimeters, points, or inches. To set the units of the rulers, choose Modify, Document, to open the Document Properties dialog box. Select a unit from the Ruler Units list, and click OK.

Do it! ## A-1: Drawing lines

Here's how	Here's why
1 Start Flash	Choose Start, Programs, Macromedia, Macromedia Flash MX.
2 Increase the size of the document to 100%	If necessary.
Close all the Panels	(Right-click the title bar of the panels, choose Close Panel.) To view the entire Stage.
Maximize the window	If necessary.
3 Choose **View, Rulers**	(To make the rulers visible.) The rulers appear along the top and left side of the work area. The origin of the ruler lies at the upper-left corner of the Stage. You can move the Toolbox to the right if the left ruler is not visible.
4 Choose **Modify, Document...**	(To open the Document Properties dialog box.) You'll change the scale of the ruler to inches.
From the Ruler Units list, select **Inches**	To change the scale of the ruler to inches.

5 Click **OK**

Observe the Ruler   The divisions are now in inches.

6 Click 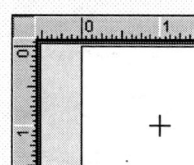   (The Line Tool is in the Toolbox.) To select the Line Tool. You'll draw straight-line segments by using the Line Tool.

7 Point as shown

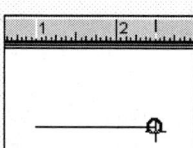

Place the pointer so that the upper ruler indicates 1 inch and the left ruler indicates 1 inch.

Drag as shown

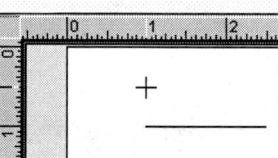

To draw a horizontal line segment. Release the mouse button when the upper ruler indicates 2.5 inches.

8 Point as shown

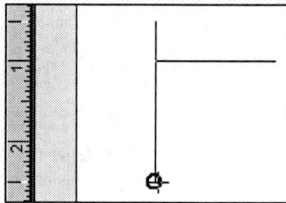

Place the pointer so that the upper ruler indicates 1 inch and the left ruler indicates 0.5 inches.

Drag as shown

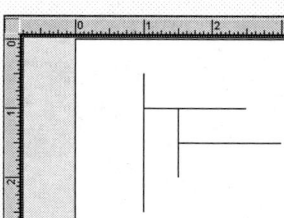

To draw a vertical line. Release the mouse button when the left ruler indicates 2.5 inches.

9 Draw two more lines as shown

Saving files

Explanation

To save a document, choose File, Save. When you save a document for the first time, the Save As dialog box appears. You need to specify the location where you want to save the file by using the Save in list to navigate to the correct folder.

You can save files in two formats: .fla or .swf. If you want to edit it later, you need to save the file in the .fla format. However, when you want to use the file on the Web, save it in the .swf format. By default, the files are stored in the Flash MX Document (*.fla) format, but you can also save them in the Flash 5 Document (*.fla) format.

Do it!

A-2:   Saving a file

Here's how	Here's why
1 Choose **File, Save**	To open the Save As dialog box.
2 From the Save in list, select the current unit folder	
3 Edit the File name box to read **My_basic_shapes**	
4 Observe the Save as type list	Flash MX Document (*.fla) is selected by default.
5 Click **Save**	To save the file.

The Rectangle Tool

Explanation

To create rectangles and squares by using the Rectangle Tool:
1   Select the Rectangle Tool.
2   Place the insertion point where you want to start drawing the rectangle.
3   Drag diagonally, until the rectangle is the size you want.

To draw a square, hold down the Shift key while dragging.

You can also use the Rectangle Tool to create rectangles and squares with rounded corners. To create a rounded rectangle by using the Rectangle Tool:
1   Click the Rectangle Tool. The Round Rectangle Radius modifier appears in the Options section of the Toolbox.
2   Click the Round Rectangle Radius modifier to open the Rectangle Settings dialog box. In the dialog box, specify the Corner Radius and click OK.
3   Place the insertion point where you want to start drawing the rectangle.
4   Drag diagonally, until the rectangle is the size you want.

Do it!   **A-3:   Creating rectangles**

Here's how	Here's why
1 Click	(The Rectangle Tool is in the Toolbox.) To select the Rectangle Tool.
2 Place the pointer at 4, 0.5	 You'll draw a rectangle whose upper-left corner lies at this point.
Drag towards the lower-right corner of the Stage until 5.5, 1	 Release the mouse button when the upper ruler indicates 5.5 and the left ruler indicates 1.
3 In the Options section, click as shown	 To open the Rectangle Settings dialog box. You can specify the corner radius for a round rectangle in the dialog box. By default, the box contains 0.
In the Corner Radius box, enter **12**	To specify the corner radius as 12 points.
Click **OK**	To close the Rectangle Settings dialog box.
4 Draw a rectangle from 6, 0.5 to 7.5, 1	The rectangle is drawn with curved corners.
5 Update the file	Choose File, Save.

The Oval Tool

Explanation

To draw ovals and circles by using the Oval Tool:

1   Select the Oval Tool.
2   Place the insertion point where you want to start drawing the oval.
3   Drag diagonally, until the oval is of the size you need.

To draw a circle, hold down the Shift key while dragging.

Do it!

A-4:   Creating ovals and circles

Here's how	Here's why
1 Click ⬜	(The Oval Tool is in the Toolbox.) To select the Oval Tool.
2 Place the pointer at 5.5, 1.5	You'll draw an oval from this point.
Drag until 7, 2	
3 Place the pointer at 2, 2	You'll draw a circle by using the Oval Tool.
4 Press (SHIFT) , and drag until 3.5, 3.5	To draw a circle.
5 Update the file	

The Pen Tool

Explanation

You use the Pen Tool to draw Bezier paths. A *Bezier path* is any straight or curved line. By using the Pen Tool, you can create an open path or a closed path. An *open path* is a straight or curved line whose start and end points do not meet. A *closed path* is one whose start and end points lie on one another, making it a closed loop. For example, a rectangle, ellipse, square, and polygon are closed paths, and a spiral is an open path. Exhibit 2-1shows a path and its various components.

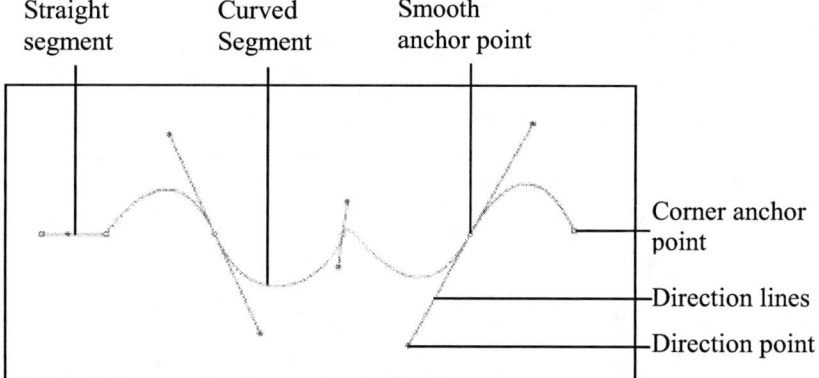

Straight segment   Curved Segment   Smooth anchor point

Corner anchor point

Direction lines

Direction point

Exhibit 2-1: A path and its components

A path created by using the Pen Tool consists of segments and anchor points. The following table describes the various components of a path:

Component	Description
Segment	The smallest building block of a path. It could be a straight or a curved line.
Anchor point	Defines the end points of a segment. It is a small, square, box-like point that links two segments to create a path. It contributes to the sharpness, smoothness, and direction of curves and lines. Anchor points are of two types: smooth and corner, which differ based on direction lines and direction points. A good image should have a minimum number of anchor points, as a large number of anchor points on a path increase its complexity and roughness.
Direction line	Defines the height or depth, and direction of the curve. The longer the direction line, the greater is the depth or height in that direction.
Direction point	Defines the end of a direction line. It is a small circle that you can drag to increase, decrease, or move the direction line. The more you drag it away from an anchor point, the longer the direction line becomes.
Smooth anchor point	Links two curved segments such that the second curve appears to be a continuation of the first. Both direction lines at this anchor point are constrained by each other at 180 degrees. If you increase, decrease, or move one direction line, the other changes proportionally in the opposite direction, thereby maintaining the smoothness.
Corner anchor point	Joins two curved or two straight segments, or a straight and a curved segment in such a way that a pointed bump appears at that point on the path. It can have one or two, or no direction lines. The direction lines are not constrained by each other, and you can modify a segment of a path without affecting the other parts of the path.

To create a path by using the Pen Tool:

1 Select the Pen Tool. You'll notice that the shape of the pointer changes to a pen.

2 Click where you want the path to start. An anchor point appears as you click.

3 Drag the mouse in the direction that the path should follow. As you drag, the direction lines for the anchor point appear. The longer the direction line, the greater is the curve of the segment. To create a straight segment, click and release the mouse.

4 Click at a point where you want to place the end point of the segment and drag the direction line. As you click, a curved segment appears that connects the first anchor point with current one. You can adjust the curve of the segment by dragging one of the direction lines.

5 To create a closed path, click the first anchor point and drag to adjust the curve. As you click, a curved segment appears that connects the last anchor point with first.

Do it!

A-5: Using the Pen Tool

Here's how	Here's why
1 Click [pen icon]	(The Pen Tool is in the Toolbox.) To select the Pen Tool. You can use the Pen Tool to create curves.
2 Point as shown	
Click and drag the pointer as shown	
	Drag the pointer towards the lower-right edge of the Stage. As you drag the pointer, two line segments appear on opposite sides of the small circle. These are the direction lines.
Release the left mouse button	

3 Point as shown

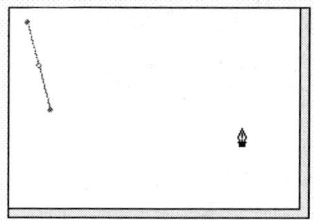

Near the lower-right corner of the Stage.

Click and drag as shown

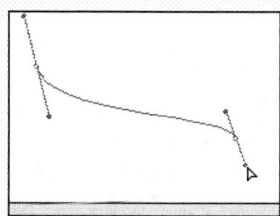

Drag toward the lower-right corner of the Stage. As you drag the direction line, the line segment connecting the two anchor points curves accordingly.

Release the left mouse button

4 Point as shown

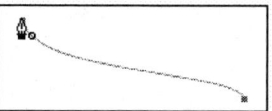

Do not release the mouse button.

5 Click and drag as shown

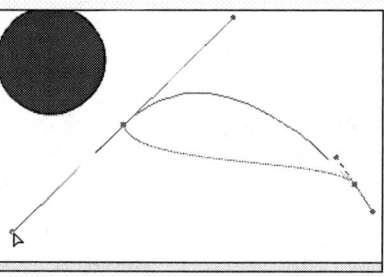

Drag towards the lower-left corner of the Stage.

Release the left mouse button

Observe the shape

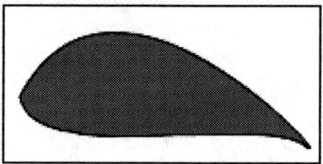

The leaf is created as shown.

6 Update the file

The Pencil Tool

Explanation   To use the Pencil Tool to create freeform shapes:

1   Select the Pencil Tool from the Toolbox. The Pencil Mode modifier appears in the Options section.
2   Select one of the options from the Pencil Mode list.
3   Place the pointer at a position where you want to start drawing the shape.
4   Drag the pointer to draw the outline of a shape.

You can use the Properties panel to define the style, height, and color of the lines created by using the Pencil Tool.

The following table describes each option in the Pencil Mode modifier:

Modifier	Description
Straighten	Used to draw straight lines. This tool also helps you create perfect basic shapes, such as triangles, circles and rectangles, from the rough outlines of these shapes.
Smooth	Used to create smooth curves and lines. This modifier smoothes the rough curves that you draw.
Ink	Used to create different shapes without any modifications being applied. Thus the shapes appear exactly as you created them.

Do it!   **A-6:   Creating freeform shapes**

Here's how	Here's why
1 Click	(The Pencil Tool is in the Toolbox.) To select the Pencil Tool.
2 In the Options section, click	A drop-down list of the pencil modes appears.
3 From the Pencil Mode list, select **Smooth**	To smoothen the shapes that you create by using the Pencil Tool.
4 Point as shown	
Drag as shown	
5 Observe the line	The sharp edges of the line are now smooth.
Draw five more lines as shown	
6 Update the file	

Topic B: Selecting shapes

Explanation

You need to select shapes to modify or move them. Flash provides three tools for selecting a shape: Arrow Tool, Subselection Tool, and Lasso Tool.

Making regular selection

You can select a shape in various ways by using the Arrow Tool. For example, you can use the Arrow Tool to select only the fill of the shape or only its stroke or both. *Stroke* is the outline of a shape. To use the Arrow Tool select:

- **Only the stroke of a shape**: Double-click the stroke of the shape. You can also select only one segment by clicking the segment.
- **Only the fill**: Click the fill of the shape.
- **The entire shape**: Double-click the fill of the shape.
- **Multiple shapes or strokes of multiple shapes**: Hold down the Shift key and select each shape or stroke individually.

The Subselection Tool

You can use the Subselection Tool to display the anchor points of a shape that was drawn by using the Rectangle, Oval, or Pencil Tool. You can then use these anchor points to change the appearance of the shape. For example, you can drag one of the direction lines from a rounded rectangle to make it a little curved at the lower side. To use the Subselection Tool, select the tool and click a shape to display the anchor points.

Making marquee selections

You can also use the Arrow Tool or Subselection Tool to make rectangular marquee selections. *Marquee selections* help you select multiple shapes or only those parts of a shape that you need to modify. To make a rectangular marquee selection:

1 Select the Arrow Tool or the Subselection Tool.
2 Place the pointer at a position where you want the selection to start.
3 Drag the pointer to cover all the shapes that you want to select. As you drag the pointer, a blank rectangle appears around the selected area.
4 Release the mouse where you want the selection to stop. The rectangle disappears and the shapes contained in it are selected.

Do it!   **B-1: Using the Arrow Tool**

Here's how	Here's why
1 Click [arrow icon]	(The Arrow Tool is in the Toolbox.) To select the Arrow Tool. You'll make various selections by using the Arrow Tool and observe the difference.
2 Click as shown	Only this line is selected.
Press (ESC)	To deselect the line.
3 Point as shown	
Double-click and observe	All four lines are now selected.
Press (ESC)	
4 Point as shown	
Drag the pointer as shown	(To create a marquee selection.) As you drag the pointer, a rectangle appears around the area.

Observe the shapes

When you release the mouse button, white dots appear over the shapes indicating that they are selected.

Press (ESC)   To deselect the shapes.

5 Select [▯]   (The Subselection Tool is in the Toolbox.) To select the Subselection Tool.

Point as shown

Click the circle

The anchor points of the circle appear.

Deselect the shape   Press the Esc key.

6 Update the file

Irregular selections

Explanation   You can also make a freeform marquee selection to select specific shapes from a cluster of shapes. For example, you want to select a single leaf from a bunch of leaves, as shown in Exhibit 2-2. Here, you cannot use the rectangle marquee selection. You use the Lasso Tool to make freeform selection.

To make a freeform marquee selection:

1 Select the Lasso Tool. The shape of the pointer changes to a lasso.
2 Place the pointer at a position where you want the selection to start.
3 Drag the pointer to draw a line around the shapes you want to select.
4 Complete the selection by connecting the starting and ending points of the line. Otherwise, Flash automatically draws a straight line between the end points.

Exhibit 2-2: The shape of a leaf selected with the Lasso Tool

Do it!

B-2:   Using the Lasso Tool

Here's how	Here's why
1 Click [⌇]	(The Lasso Tool is in the Toolbox.) To select the Lasso Tool.
2 Point as shown	
	The pointer changes to the shape of a lasso.
Drag as shown	
	As you drag the pointer, a line is drawn. When you release the pointer, the shapes that are surrounded by this line are selected.

3 Choose **Window**, **Properties**	To open the Properties panel.
4 In the Properties panel, click as shown	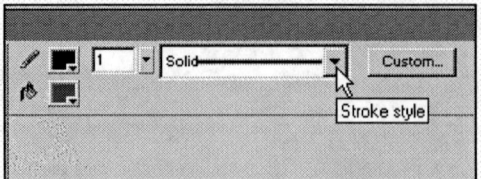
From the Stroke Style list, select as shown	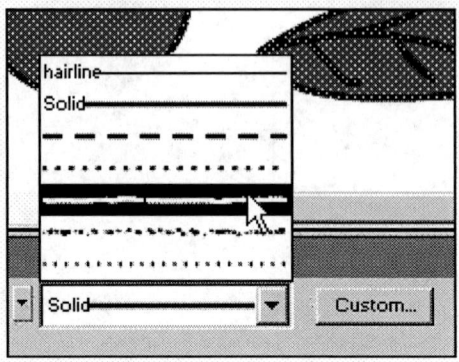
	To change the line style to wavy.
Close the Properties panel	
5 Select the Arrow Tool	To deselect the Lasso Tool.
Deselect the shapes	
6 Update and close the file	

Topic C: Viewing and editing shapes

Explanation

You can view a document at different levels of detail by using the Zoom Tool or the Hand Tool. You can transform an existing shape to a new shape by using the Arrow Tool or the Eraser Tool.

Viewing shapes

You can view a document in three modes: Zoom In, Zoom Out, and Magnification. You can use Zoom In and Zoom Out to view a specific part of a document in magnified or reduced form. You can use Magnification to view the entire document in a magnified form.

When you use a viewing tool, only the display of the shape is altered and not its dimensions or file size. You can select magnification levels ranging from 25% to 800%, or you can specify your own magnification level. The percentage of a shape's actual size appears in the Zoom box.

The Zoom Tool

While creating a shape, you can have a closer look at it by zooming in so that you can work on the details. You can then reduce the size of the shape to view the entire document by zooming out. To do this, you use the Zoom Tool. When you select the Zoom Tool, the Enlarge and Reduce modifiers appear in the Options section of the Toolbox. By default, the Enlarge modifier is selected.

You can zoom into or magnify a shape by selecting the Zoom Tool and then clicking the shape. To reduce the size of the shape, select the Reduce modifier and then click the shape.

The Hand Tool

After you have zoomed in on a shape, you can see only some parts of the document. However, you can move the Stage to view the other components of the document. You can use the Hand Tool for moving the Stage.

To move the Stage, select the Hand Tool and drag the Stage in the direction you want to move it.

Do it!

C-1: Viewing shapes

Here's how	Here's why
1 Open Editing shapes	(From the current unit folder.) The document opens with a magnification of 100%.
2 Double-click [hand icon]	(The Hand Tool is in the View section of the Toolbox.) The document now appears in the Show Frame mode so that you are able to view the entire document.
3 Click [zoom icon]	(The Zoom Tool is in the View section of the Toolbox.) The pointer changes to a magnifying glass with a plus (+) sign.
4 Click the oval shape	The oval is visible in the magnified form.

5 Switch to Show Frame view	Double-click the Hand Tool icon on the Toolbox.
6 Save the file as **My_editing_shapes**	In the current unit folder.

Editing the curves and corners of a shape

Explanation

You can change the appearance of basic shapes by using the Arrow Tool and Free Transform Tool. For example, you can create the shape of a mango from an oval by pulling one of its sides inward, or you can create the shape of a diamond by editing the corners of a rectangle by using the Free Transform Tool.

To edit the curves and corners of a shape, select the Free Transform Tool and place the pointer over the line segment that you want to reshape. A curve or a corner appears at the tail end of the pointer indicating that you can modify it. Drag the pointer to create the shape of your choice.

Arrow Tool and Free Transform Tool modifiers

When you select the Arrow Tool or the Free Transform Tool, their modifiers appear in the Options section of the Toolbox.

The following table describes the modifiers of the Arrow Tool and Free Transform Tool. The first two modifiers are enabled when you select the Arrow Tool and the rest are enabled when you select the Free Transform Tool.

Modifier	Description
	Smooth any sharp areas in the selected shape.
	Straighten any curves in the selected shape.
	Rotate the selected shape. When you select this modifier, the shape appears surrounded by small black squares called shape handles. This modifier can be selected only when a shape is selected on the Stage.
	Resize the selected shape. When you select this modifier, the shape appears surrounded by small black squares called shape handles. This modifier can be selected only when a shape is selected on the Stage.
	Distort the selected shape. When you select this modifier, the shape appears surrounded by small black squares called shape handles. This modifier can be selected only when a shape is selected on the Stage.
	Warp and distort objects. When you select this modifier, the shape appears surrounded by small white circles and squares called shape handles. Changes made by dragging the shape handles affect the shape of the objects contained within it. This modifier can be selected only when a shape is selected on the Stage.

Do it!   **C-2:   Changing the shape structure**

Here's how	**Here's why**
1 Select the Arrow Tool	
2 Point as shown	
	The shape of the pointer changes to an arrow with a curve at its tail end.
3 Drag as shown	
4 Point as shown	
Drag as shown	
5 Double-click the shape	To select the shape.
6 In the Toolbox, click	(The Free Transform Tool is in the Toolbox.) To select the Free Transform Tool.
7 In the Options section, click	You'll rotate the chili shape.
Observe the shape	
	The black squares around the shape are called shape handles. These appear only when you select the shape and the Free Transform Tool.
Point as shown	
	The shape of the pointer changes as shown.
Drag as shown	

8 In the Options section, click

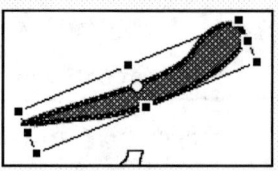

To resize the shape.

Point as shown

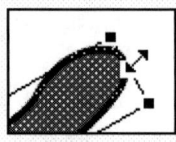

The shape of the pointer changes to a double-headed arrow.

Drag towards the lower-left corner, as shown

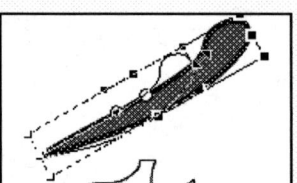

To resize the selected shape.

9 Click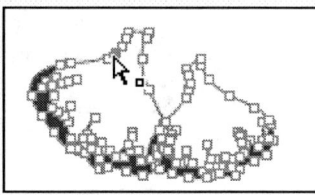

You'll make the anchor points of a shape visible and modify the shape.

Click as shown

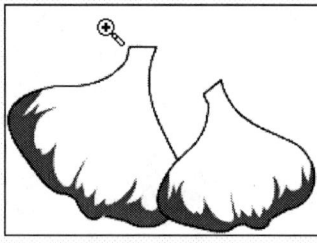

Observe the shape

The anchor points and the direction lines for the shape are now visible.

10 Select the Zoom Tool

Point as shown

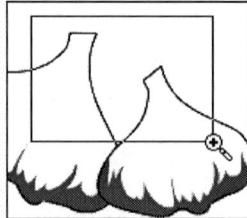

Drag as shown

11 Select the Subselection Tool	Click the Subselection Tool in the Toolbox.
12 Click as shown	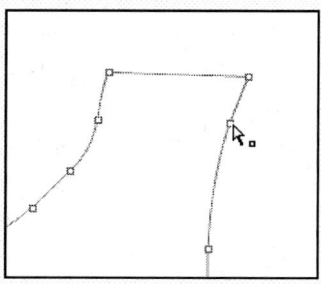
	The direction lines appear on either side of the anchor point.
13 Point as shown	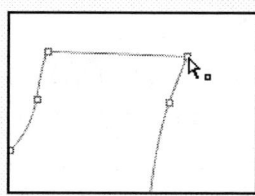
Drag as shown	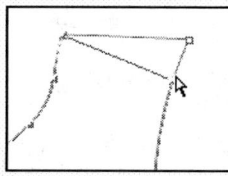
	Notice that as you drag, the stroke of the shape also moves accordingly.
14 Click anywhere on the Stage	To deselect the shape.
Double-click 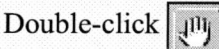	(The Hand Tool is in the Toolbox.) To change the magnification of the Stage to Show Frame.
15 Update the file	

Erasing shapes

Explanation

You can use the Eraser Tool to remove parts of a shape. When you select the Eraser Tool, its modifiers appear in the Options section of the Toolbox. There are three modifiers for the Eraser Tool:

- **The Faucet modifier** — Helps you erase the entire stroke or the fill. For example, you can use the Faucet modifier when you want to erase the fill of a rectangle but not the stroke. To use the Faucet modifier select the Eraser Tool, select the Faucet modifier, and click the portion of the shape that you want to erase.

- **The Eraser Shape modifier** — Helps you select a shape and size of the eraser from the Eraser Shape drop-down list. This helps you erase more accurately because you can choose a small size of the eraser when you want to erase small portions of a shape. Also, you can erase large areas quickly by choosing a bigger eraser.

- **The Eraser Mode modifier** — Helps you erase a particular part of a shape depending on the option that you select from the drop-down list.

The following table describes the use of various options of the Eraser Mode modifier:

Eraser mode	Description
Erase Normal	Erases any part of the shape over which you drag the pointer.
Erase Fills	Erases only the fills. Selecting this modifier does not erase any lines that are present.
Erase Lines	Erases only the strokes of a shape. Selecting this modifier does not erase any fills that are present.
Erase Selected Fills	Erases only the fills of the shape that is selected. Selecting this modifier does not erase any lines in the selected shape.
Erase Inside	Erases only the fill inside the shape where you started erasing. Any fills outside the shape are not erased when this modifier is used.

To use the Eraser Tool, select it and select values for the various options in the Options section. Then drag the pointer over the shape where you want to erase it.

Do it!   ## C-3:   Using the Eraser Tool

Here's how	Here's why
1 Draw a selection marquee as shown	Use the Arrow Tool.
2 Click	(The Eraser Tool is in the Toolbox.) To select the Eraser Tool.
3 In the Options section, click	A list containing the various Eraser modes appears.
From the Eraser Mode list, select **Erase Selected Fills**	This option allows you to erase only the fill of the shape in which you started erasing. Any fills outside the shape are not erased when this modifier is used.
4 From the Eraser Shape list, select as shown	The shape of the pointer changes to a small black square.

5 Click as shown

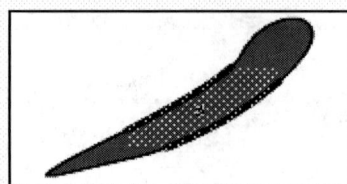

Drag as shown

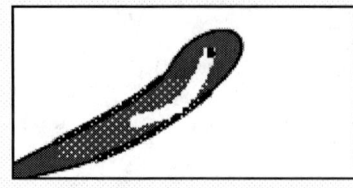

Observe the shape

Only the selected fill of the shape is erased, even if you drag the pointer over the fill that is not selected.

6 From the Eraser Mode list, select **Erase Fills**

This option lets you to erase only the fills over which you drag the pointer, without affecting any lines that are present.

From the Eraser Shape list, select as shown

7 Erase the right side fill of the shape as shown

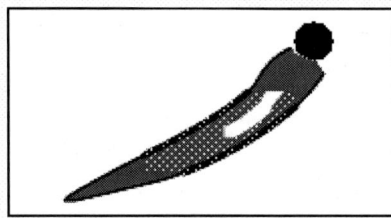

Deselect the shape

If necessary.

8 Update and close the file

Topic D: Handling shapes

Explanation

You can modify a document by creating more similar shapes, repositioning some shapes, or deleting shapes that do not fit in. To do so you need to copy, move, or delete shapes.

Copying shapes

After creating a shape, you might need to use the same shape with the same size and dimensions somewhere else in the document. You can do so by creating a copy of the shape. To create a copy of a shape:

1 Select the shape and choose Edit, Copy.

2 Choose Edit, Paste.

3 A copy of the shape appears at the center of the Stage.

Moving shapes

Moving a shape refers to changing its position on the Stage. You can move a shape by using:

- **The Arrow Tool** — Select the tool, double-click the shape and then drag to move it.
- **The keyboard arrow keys** — Select the shape and then press the arrow key corresponding to the direction in which you want to move the shape.
- **The Info panel** — Select the shape. The X and Y property cells on the Info panel are activated. Specify the value of the X position and Y position in the corresponding boxes. The shape moves to the new position.

Do it!

D-1: Copying and moving a shape

Here's how	Here's why
1 Open Handling shapes	You'll create a copy of the lines that you created.
Switch to Show Frame view	
2 Select the Arrow Tool	
3 Select as shown	

Double-click the lines.

4 Press CTRL + **C**	To create a copy of the selected shape.
5 Press CTRL + **V**	(To display the copy of the shape.) A copy of the shape appears at the center of the Stage.
6 Point as shown	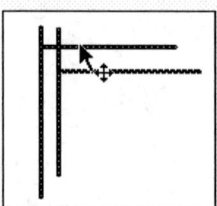
7 Drag as shown	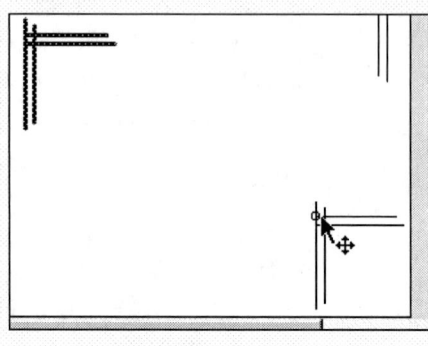

To the lower-right corner. |
| Make another copy of the lines | Press Ctrl + V. |
| 8 Verify that the Arrow Tool is selected | |
| Select the lines at the lower-right corner |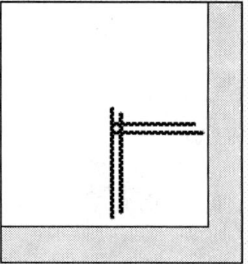

The lines that you dragged. |
| 9 Click the Free Transform Tool |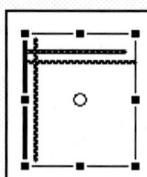

The anchor points appear. |
| Select the Rotate and Skew modifier | Point to the upper right anchor point. |

10 Rotate as shown

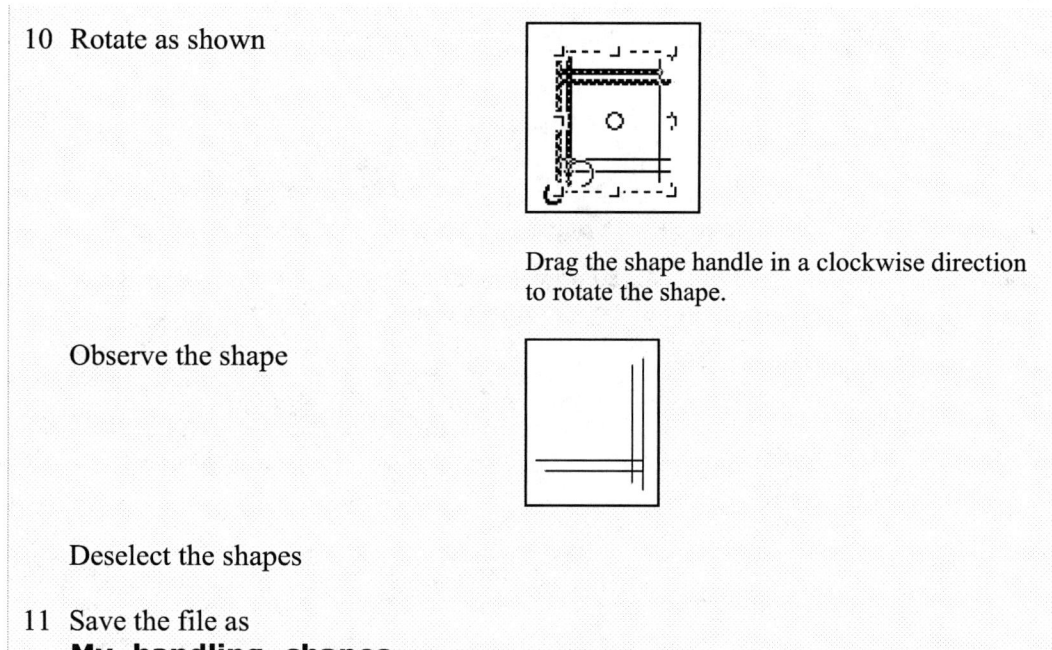

Drag the shape handle in a clockwise direction to rotate the shape.

Observe the shape

Deselect the shapes

11 Save the file as
My_handling_shapes

Deleting shapes

Explanation

To delete a shape, select it by using the Arrow Tool and choose Edit, Clear, or press the Delete key. You can delete multiple shapes by selecting all of them and then choosing Edit, Clear.

Do it!

D-2:   Deleting a shape

Here's how	Here's why
1 Select the lines at the center of the Stage, as shown	You'll delete these lines because you do not need them in your Web page.
2 Choose **Edit, Clear**	The lines are deleted from the Stage.
3 Update and close the file	

Unit summary: Creating shapes

Topic A

In this unit, you learned how to **create basic shapes** by using the **drawing tools**. You also learned how to use the **Line Tool** to create lines, **the Rectangle Tool** to create squares and rectangles, and the **Oval Tool** to create ovals and circles. You also learned how to use the **Pencil Tool** to create freeform shapes and the **Pen Tool** to create curves.

Topic B

Next, you learned how to **select shapes**. You also learned how to use the **Arrow Tool** for marquee selection, the **Subselection Tool** to select anchor points, the **Lasso Tool** to select irregular shapes, and the **Free Transform Tool** to modify shapes.

Topic C

Then, you learned how to **view** and **edit shapes**. You learned how to use the **Zoom Tool** to view a shape in a magnified form and the **Hand Tool** to bring the shape back to its original size. You also learned how to use the **Arrow Tool**, the **Subselection Tool**, and the **Free Transform Tool** to change the structure of a shape, and the **Eraser Tool** to erase parts of a shape.

Topic D

Finally, you learned how to **handle shapes**. You also learned how to **Copy**, **Move**, and **Delete** Shapes.

Independent practice activity

1 Open **Basic shapes practice** from the current unit folder.

2 Use the Oval Tool to draw a circle big enough to include five leaves and a stem.

3 Create four copies of the leaf. (Hint: Move each leaf from the center of the Stage.)

4 Use the Pencil Tool to create the shape of a stem.

5 Use the Line Tool to create three lines.

6 Rotate and position the stem, the leaves, and the lines, as shown in Exhibit 2-3.

7 Save the file as **My_basic_shapes_practice**.

8 Close the file.

Exhibit 2-3: The position of shapes after step 6 of the Independent Practice Activity

Unit 3

Working with colors

Unit time: 60 minutes

Complete this unit, and you'll know how to:

A Apply stroke and fill colors to a shape by using the Paint Bucket, Ink Bottle, and Eyedropper tools.

B Create custom colors, swatches, and line styles.

Topic A: Applying colors

Explanation

A simple shape can have a lot of flair. For example, it can have various stroke styles, stroke colors and fill colors. To apply a stroke or fill color to a shape, first you need to select the color from the Colors section of the Toolbox. Then you can use tools such as the Paint Bucket, Ink Bottle, Eyedropper, or Brush to apply the colors.

Colors section

The Colors section contains the Stroke Color box and the Fill Color box. Also, the three buttons near the lower edge of the Colors section, shown in Exhibit 3-1, help you to modify the color settings of shapes.

By default, the stroke color is black and the fill color is blue. When you create a new shape, it has the same stroke and fill colors that were last selected from the Fill and the Stroke color palettes.

You can use the Colors section to:

- **Specify the stroke color of a shape.** Select a shape, click the Stroke Color box to display the Stroke Color palette, and select the stroke color of your choice.
- **Specify the fill color of a shape.** Select a shape, click the Fill Color box to display the Fill Color palette, and select the fill color of your choice.
- **Swap the fill and stroke colors.** Click the Swap Colors button at the lower-right corner of the Colors section. *Swapping* interchanges the fill and the stroke colors of the selected shape.
- **Revert to the default colors.** Click the Black and White button at the lower-left corner of the Colors section to change the stroke color to black, and fill color to white.
- **Create a shape having no fill or stroke color.** Click the Fill Color box or the Stroke Color box. Click the No color button next to the Black and White button to create a shape with no fill or stroke color.

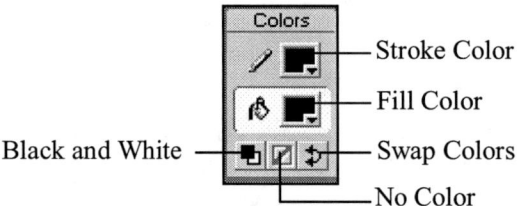

Exhibit 3-1: The Colors section

The colors in the color palette appear in the form of tiles called *swatches*. To apply a color to a shape, select a swatch from the color palette or specify the hexadecimal value for the color in the box at the upper part of the color palette.

Hexadecimal values

Hexadecimal values are based on the base-16 number system. The sequence of numbers in this number system is 0-9 followed by letters from A-F. Here, 0-9 represents the first 10 numbers in the decimal number system and A-F represents numbers from 10-15.

The box in the color palette shows the hexadecimal value in the "#XXXXXX" format. Here, # indicates that the number is hexadecimal. In addition, the first two Xs represent the amount of red color, the next two Xs represent the amount of green color, and the last two Xs represent the amount of blue color. The resulting color is a combination of all these colors. The following table shows some commonly used colors and their hexadecimal values:

Color name	Hexadecimal value
Black	#000000
White	#FFFFFF
Red	#FF0000
Yellow	#FFFF00
Green	#00FF00
Blue	#0000FF

Gradient swatches

The Fill Color box also contains the gradient swatches. A *gradient* is a smooth transition between two or more colors, where one color blends into another color. You can apply gradients to fills, but you cannot apply them to strokes.

The Paint Bucket Tool

You use the Paint Bucket Tool to apply fill color to a shape. To use this tool:

1   Select the Paint Bucket Tool, and select the option you want from the Options section, if needed.
2   Click the Fill Color box in the Colors section of the Toolbox to display the Fill Color palette and select the color of your choice.
3   Click inside the shape to which you want to apply the fill color.

When you select the Paint Bucket Tool, two modifiers appear in the Options section: Gap Size and Lock Fill. The following table describes the use of each modifier:

Modifier	Description
Gap Size	Adds color to a shape that is not closed and has small gaps. When you click this modifier, a list appears containing various options for the gap size. These options help you to add color to a shape depending on the size of the gap between the start and the end point of the shape.
Lock Fill	Adds gradient color to a shape in such a way that the gradient color appears to be stretched across the shape.

Do it!

A-1: Using the Paint Bucket Tool

Here's how	Here's why
1 Open Using colors	(From the current unit folder.) This file contains various shapes that you'll be using for the Web page.
Double-click the Hand Tool	To view the file in Show Frame view.
2 Click	(The Paint Bucket Tool is in the Toolbox.) You'll change the fill color of the shapes.
3 Click as shown	To display the Fill Color palette.
4 Select as shown	(# 003300 swatch.) To select the black color. The shape of the pointer changes to an Eyedropper.

5 Point as shown

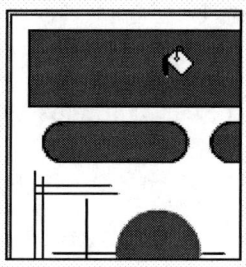

   Click and observe the rectangle   The color of the rectangle changes to black.

6 Display the Fill Color palette   In the Colors section of the Toolbox, click Fill Color box.

7 In the Fill Color palette, click as shown

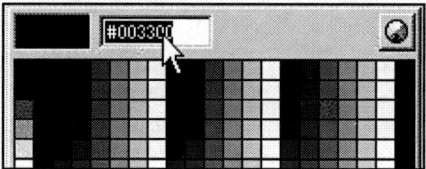

   You'll specify a hexadecimal value for the red color.

   In the box, enter **#FF0000**   This is the hexadecimal value for the red color that you'll apply to the chili.

   Press ⤶ ENTER   Notice that the color in the Fill Color box changes to red.

8 Point as shown

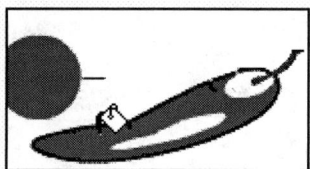

   The chili near the left edge of the Stage.

   Click and observe the chili   The color of the chili changes to red.

9 Change the blue fill of both the garlic shapes to #FFCCFF   Verify that the Paint Bucket Tool is selected. Display the Fill Color palette and in the box, enter #FFCCFF. Press Enter and click the blue fill inside the garlic shape.

10 Save the file as **My_using_colors**   In the current unit folder.

The Ink Bottle Tool

Explanation

You use the Ink Bottle Tool to apply stroke color to a shape. To use this tool:

1 Select the Ink Bottle Tool.
2 Click the Stroke Color box in the Colors section of the Toolbox to display the Stroke Color palette and select the color of your choice.
3 Click the shape to which you want to apply the stroke color.

Do it!

A-2: Using the Ink Bottle Tool

Here's how	Here's why
1 Click	To select the Ink Bottle Tool.
2 Click as shown	To display the Stroke Color palette.
3 In the Stroke Color palette, in the box, enter **#CC0000** Press ⏎ ENTER	This is the hexadecimal value for the dark red color.
4 Click as shown	The stroke color of the chili changes to dark red.
5 Select the Zoom Tool Zoom in on the lines near the lower-right corner of the Stage	(Scroll down, if necessary.) To view the lines clearly.
6 Select the Arrow Tool Select the lines	(Double-click the lines.) You'll change the stroke color of the lines.

7 Select the Ink Bottle Tool	
In the Stroke Color palette, enter **#996600**	The color of the lines changes to brown.
Press (↵ ENTER)	
Select the lines in the remaining corners	You'll change their Stroke color.
Click the Ink Bottle Tool and click on any one of the lines	The colors of all the lines change to brown.
From the Stroke style list select **hairline**	If necessary.
8 Switch to Show Frame view	
Deselect the lines	
9 Update the file	

The Eyedropper Tool

Explanation

You use the Eyedropper Tool to copy the stroke or fill color of a shape so you can use it elsewhere. To use this tool to copy the stroke color:

1   Select the Eyedropper Tool and place the pointer on the outline of the shape whose stroke color you want to copy. The shape of the pointer changes to an eyedropper with a pencil at its side.
2   Click the stroke of the shape. The shape of the pointer changes to an ink bottle.
3   Click the outline of the shape to which you want to apply the stroke color.

To use this tool to copy the fill color:

1   Select the Eyedropper Tool and place the pointer inside the shape whose fill color you want to copy. The shape of the pointer changes to an eyedropper with a paintbrush at its side.
2   Click the fill of the shape. The shape of the pointer now changes to a paint bucket.
3   Click inside the shape to which you want to apply the fill color.

A-3:   Using the Eyedropper Tool

Here's how	Here's why
1 Click  ![eyedropper]	To select the Eyedropper Tool.
2 Point as shown	 A paintbrush appears on the right side of the Eyedropper.
3 Click the chili	 The shape of the pointer changes to a paint bucket with a lock.
Observe the Toolbox	The Eyedropper Tool is no longer selected. The Paint Bucket Tool is now selected.
4 Click as shown	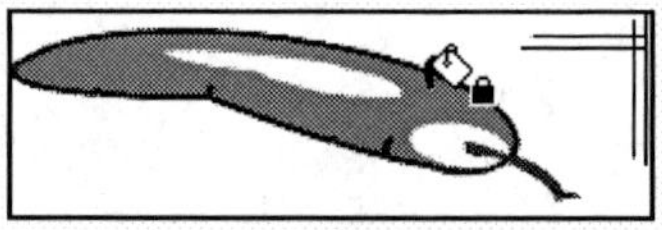 (The chili on the right side of the Stage.) The fill of the chili changes to red.
5 Select the Eyedropper Tool	Click the Eyedropper Tool in the Toolbox.
6 Point as shown	 (To select the stroke color of the chili.) A pencil appears on the right side of the eyedropper.
7 Click the stroke of the chili	 The shape of the pointer changes to an ink bottle.
Observe the Toolbox	The Eyedropper Tool is no longer selected. The Ink Bottle Tool is now selected.

8 Click as shown

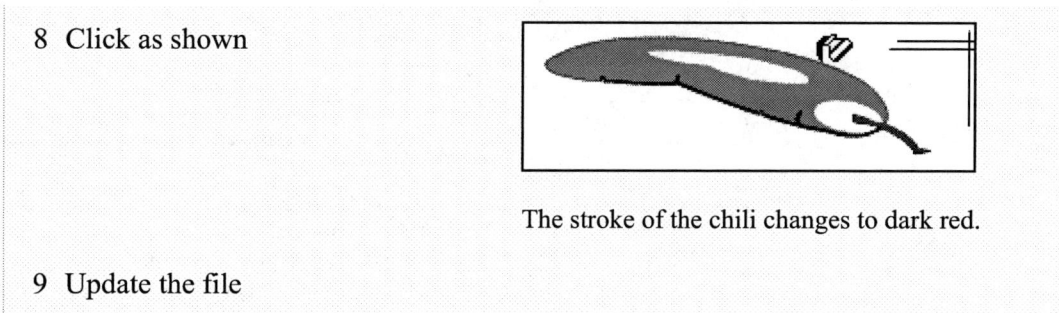

The stroke of the chili changes to dark red.

9 Update the file

The Brush Tool

Explanation

You use the Brush Tool to add brush-like strokes to an image, as shown in Exhibit 3-2. After you select the tool, you can change the size and shape of the brush by selecting the various options for the modifiers available in the Options section of the Toolbox.

Brush strokes applied to give the effect of background

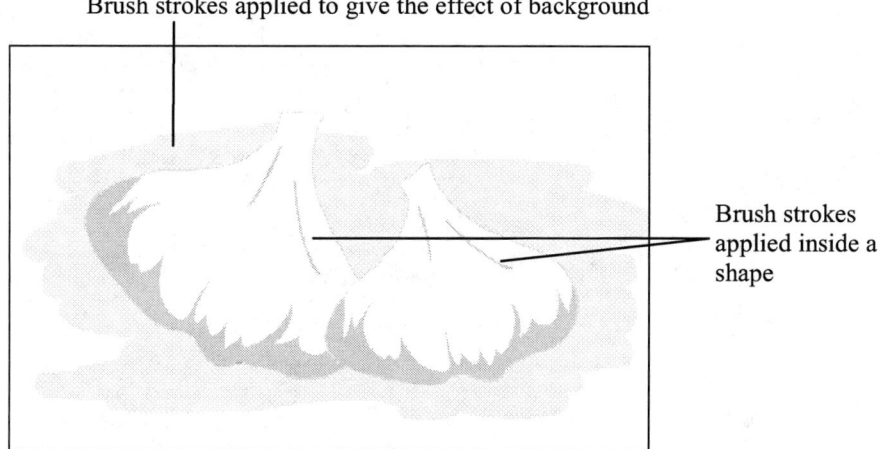

Brush strokes applied inside a shape

Exhibit 3-2: The use of the Brush Tool to add special effects to an image

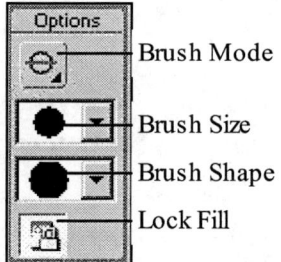

Brush Mode

Brush Size

Brush Shape

Lock Fill

Exhibit 3-3: The modifiers for the Brush Tool

The following table describes the different types of modifiers for the Brush Tool, as shown in Exhibit 3-3:

Modifier	Description
Brush Mode	Choose the type of strokes that you want to create. When you click this modifier, a list containing the options for the brush mode appears. The Brush Tool paints:
	• Any strokes or fills over which you drag the mouse when you select the Paint Normal option. You use this option when you want the brush stokes to appear above all the strokes or fills in the area over which you drag the mouse.
	• Only the fills over which you drag the mouse when you select the Paint Fills option. You use this option when you want the brush strokes to appear only above the fill color of a shape without affecting the outlines.
	• Only the area behind the filled shapes, when you select the Paint Behind option. You use this option when you want the brush strokes to appear as the background of the shape.
	• Only the selected parts of an image when you select the Paint Selection option. You use this option when you want the brush strokes to appear only above the fill or stroke color of only those areas that you select. The brush strokes are not applied to any area that is outside the selected area.
	• Only those areas having the same color, when you select the Paint Inside option.
Brush Size	Specifies the brush size.
Brush Shape	Specifies the brush shape.
Lock Fill	Adds brush strokes with gradient colors to a shape in such a way that the gradient color appears to be stretching across the shape.

Do it!

A-4: Using the Brush Tool

Here's how	Here's why
1 Click	(To select the Brush Tool.) The shape of the pointer changes to a black circle.
2 Change the fill color to #FFCCFF	
3 In the Options section, click	To display the Brush Mode list.
From the Brush Mode list, select **Paint Fills**	You'll only paint the fills, without affecting the outline.

4   From the Brush Size list, select as shown

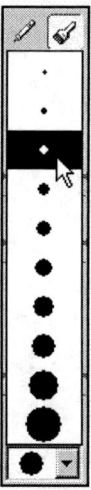

5   From the Brush Shape list, select as shown

6   Point as shown

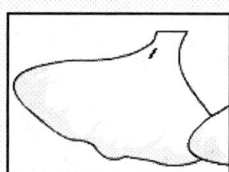

The shape of the pointer changes to a small line tilted at an angle.

7   Click and drag as shown

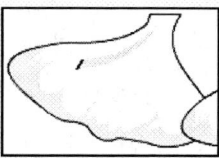

Apply more brush strokes as shown

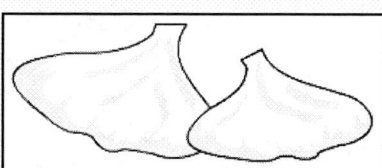

8   Update the file

Topic B: Creating custom colors, gradients, and line styles

To use colors or gradients other than those available in the Fill Color palette or the Stroke Color palette, you can create custom colors and gradients and save them. You can also create Stroke styles with specific attributes, such as thickness, color, and patterns, that are not available by default, and also save them for later use.

Custom colors

You can create a new custom color in all the color modes that Flash provides. A *color mode* defines the process by which colors arc created for printing and displaying on a screen.

Color modes

There are three color modes in Flash: RGB, HSB, and Hex. The following table describes these color modes:

Color Mode	Description
RGB (Red, Green, Blue)	Based upon light emissions, that is, how a light appears when mixed with a light of another color. They are known as additive colors because you can mix these colors to get a different color. Their values range from 0 to 255, where 0 represents black, 255 represents white, and all other colors lie in between them according to their lightness or darkness.
HSB (Hue, Saturation, Brightness)	Based on the way humans view colors, that is according to the name of the color (hue), the intensity and purity of that color (saturation), and its luminosity (brightness).
Hex (Hexadecimal)	Based on the Hexadecimal numbers whose values are equivalent to RGB colors.

Color Mixer panel

You use the Color Mixer panel to create a custom color. To create a custom color:

1   Select a color from the Fill Color or Stroke Color palette in the Color Mixer panel. You can also select a color from the Color selector bar in the Color Mixer panel.

2   Click the triangle on the upper-right corner of the Color Mixer panel to display the Options menu. From the menu, choose a color mode. Depending on the color mode that you select, the values in the R, G, B, and Alpha boxes change.

3   Edit the values in the R, G, B, and Alpha boxes to create a new color.

4   From the Options menu, choose Add Swatch. The color is saved in the Fill Color palette if you selected a color from the Fill Color palette. It is saved in the Stroke Color palette if you selected a color from the Stroke Color palette.

Do it!   **B-1:   Creating a custom fill color**

Here's how	Here's why
1 Select the Arrow Tool	
Select as shown	
2 Choose **Window, Color Mixer**	To display the Color Mixer panel.
3 In the Color Mixer panel, click the Fill Color box	To display the Fill Color palette.
4 Change the color to #996633	
Observe the values in the R, G, B, and Alpha boxes in the Mixer panel	The values in the R, G, and B boxes represent the amount of the red, green, and blue color respectively, in the selected color. The value in the Alpha box represents the percentage of transparency of the selected color.
5 Click as shown	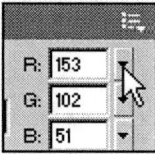
	To display the red color slider.
Observe the Color Mixer panel	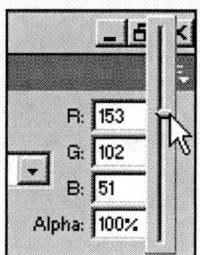
	The slider for the red color appears.
Drag the slider downwards, as shown	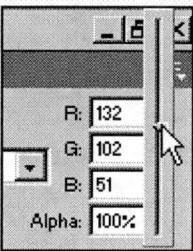
	Drag until the value in the R box is 132.
Click anywhere in the Color Mixer panel	To close the red color slider.

6 Change the value in the G box to 113	Click the triangle next to the G box to display the color slider. Drag the slider upwards so that the value in the G box is 113. Click anywhere in the Mixer panel to close the color slider.
Change the value in the B box to 125	Drag the slider upwards.
Change the value in the Alpha box to 56%	Drag the slider downwards.
7 In the Color Mixer panel, click as shown	
	To display the Options menu.
Choose **Add Swatch**	You'll save the new color.
Click anywhere on the Stage	The rectangles have the new fill color.
8 Update the file	

Custom gradients

Explanation   You can use the Color Mixer panel to create a custom gradient. To create a custom gradient:

1 From the Fill style list, select a gradient type. There are two types of gradients:

- Linear — The transition of the colors is linear across a shape.
- Radial — The transition of colors occurs in a circular form in the shape.

2 The gradient bar, gradient slider, and the Gradient sample box appear below the Fill style list. You can adjust the position of the various sliders by moving them. As you move the sliders, a new gradient is created and a preview of the new gradient appears in the Gradient sample box.

3 Display the Options menu and choose Add Swatch. The gradient is added to the Fill Color palette.

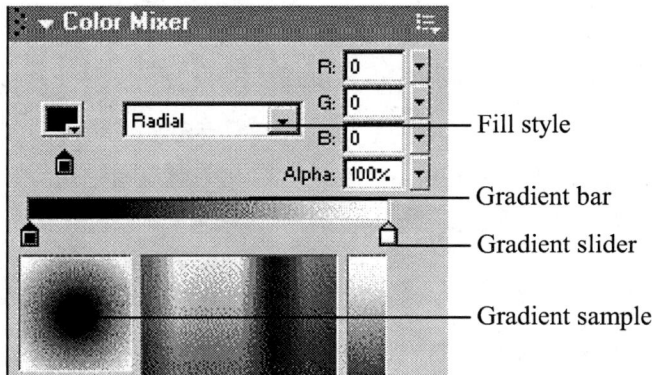

Exhibit 3-4: The Color Mixer panel

Do it!   ## B-2:   Creating a custom gradient

Here's how	Here's why
1 Select the circle	You'll create a new gradient color for this circle.
2 In the Color Mixer panel, click as shown	A list of fill style options appears.
From the list, select **Radial**	A black and white sample gradient and the gradient slider appear as shown in Exhibit 3-4.
3 Click as shown	To display the gradient color palette.
Change the gradient color to #FF9900	

4 Click as shown

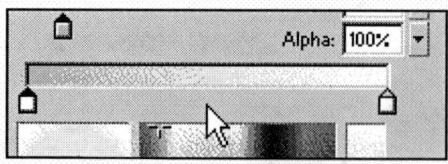

Observe the Color Mixer panel

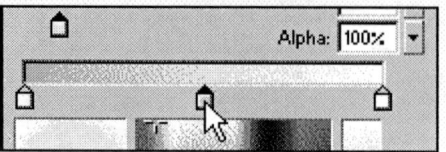

A new slider appears where you clicked.

Change the gradient color to #FF0000

To change the color of the new gradient slider to red.

5 Click as shown

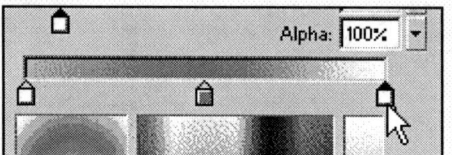

Change the gradient color to #FFFF66

6 Display the Options menu

Click the white arrow at the upper-right corner of the Color Mixer panel.

Choose **Add Swatch**

To save the gradient in the Fill Color palette.

Deselect the circle

The circle has the new gradient as its fill color.

7 Click the Fill color palette in the Colors section of Tools

Point as shown

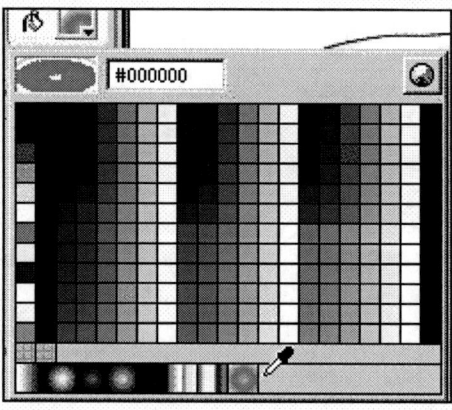

This is the new swatch that you added.

8 Close the Color Mixer panel

9 Update the file

Custom line styles

Explanation
To create custom line styles:

1 Choose, the Line Tool, choose Window, Properties.

2 In the Properties panel, click Custom. The Stroke Style dialog box appears, as shown in Exhibit 3-5.

3 Set the values for the various options to create a line style of your choice. A preview of the stroke style appears in the Preview box.

4 Click OK to create the custom stroke style. This stroke style is added to the stroke style list in the Properties panel.

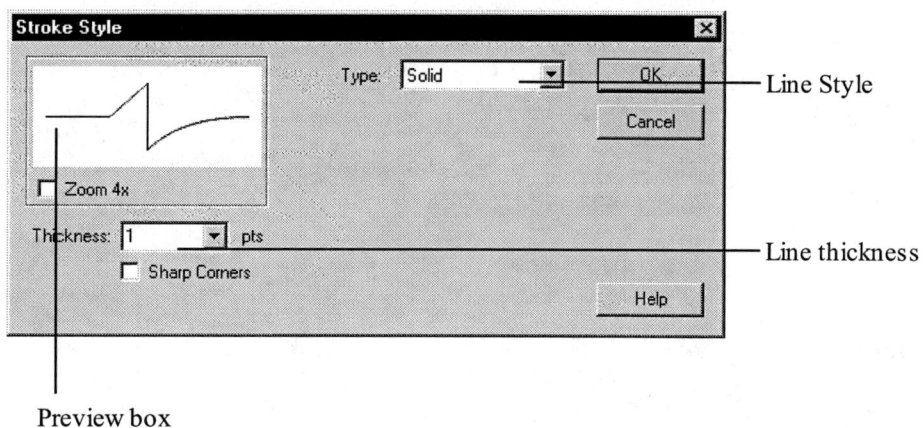

Preview box

Exhibit 3-5: The Stroke Style dialog box

Do it!
B-3: Creating a custom stroke style

Here's how	Here's why
1 Choose **Windows, Properties**	To display the Properties panel.
2 Select the Line Tool	You'll draw four lines.
3 In the Properties panel click **Custom**	To display the Stroke Style dialog box.
4 From the Thickness list, select **2**	The thickness of the stroke in the Preview box changes.
5 From the Type list, select **Ragged**	Type: Ragged Pattern: Simple Wave Height: Wavy Wave Length: Short Notice that three more list boxes appear.

6 From the Pattern list, select **Random Dotted**

To specify a pattern for the new stroke style.

From the Wave Height list, select **Very Wavy**

To specify the height of waves on the new stroke style.

From the Wave Length list, select **Very Short**

To specify the length of the waves in the new stroke style.

7 Observe the Preview box

A preview of the new stroke style appears.

Click **OK**

In the Properties panel, observe the Stroke style list

The new stroke style is added to the stroke style list.

8 In the Properties panel, change the Stroke color to #996600

To change the color to brown.

Close the Properties panel

9 Draw a line as shown

(Drag the pointer on the Stage.) The line has the same style that you created.

Draw the remaining lines as shown

10 Update and close the file

Unit summary: Working with colors

Topic A   In this unit, you learned how to use the **Fill Color** box and the **Stroke Color** box. You learned how to apply **fill color** and **stroke color** to a shape by using the **Paint Bucket Tool** and the **Ink Bottle Tool** respectively. You also learned how to use the **Eyedropper Tool** to **copy** the **fill** and **stroke color** of one shape to another. Then, you learned to use the **Brush Tool** to add brush-like strokes to shapes.

Topic B   Finally, you learned how to **create** and **save custom colors**, **swatches**, and **line styles** by using the **Color Mixer panel**, the **Properties panel**, and the **Stroke Style dialog box**.

Independent practice activity

1 Open **Colors practice**.

2 Change the stroke color of the lines at the upper-left corner of the Stage to **#660033**.

3 Change the fill color of the leaf below the lines to **#00CC33**. (Hint: Use the marquee selection to select the leaf.)

4 Deselect the leaf.

5 By using the Eye Dropper Tool, copy the light green color of the leaf below the lines to all the other leaves.

6 Select the circle.

7 Display the Color Mixer panel.

8 Create a new Linear gradient with **#3366FF**(Blue), **#FFFF66** (Yellow), **#33FF00**(Green), and **#CC9966** (Brown).

9 Deselect the circle and close the Color Mixer panel.

10 From the Fill Color palette, select the **#CC00CC** swatch.

11 Select the Brush Tool and from Brush Mode list, select Paint Behind. Change the brush size to a larger size and the brush shape to a thicker style.

12 Apply brush strokes over the two garlic shapes, as shown in Exhibit 3-6.

13 Save the file as **My_colors_practice**.

14 Close the file.

Exhibit 3-6: The Stage after step 12 of the Independent Practice Activity

Unit 4

Manipulating shapes and images

Unit time: 50 minutes

Complete this unit, and you'll know how to:

A Combine and group shapes.

B Import raster images and convert them to vector images.

Topic A: Combining and grouping shapes

Explanation

Macromedia Flash MX offers features that simplify combining and grouping shapes. To combine shapes, you place one shape on top of another and the two are made into one. When you want to perform some common actions on multiple shapes, you can group them, which means that the individual shapes are treated as a single unit.

Combining shapes

When combining shapes there are two facts you need to keep in mind. First, you can only combine shapes that have the same fill color. Second, both shapes need to have no defined stroke color. As long as those two criteria are met, you can combine shapes by placing one shape over the other.

On the other hand, when you overlap shapes that have different fill colors or different stroke colors defined for them, they are not combined. Instead, the area where the shapes overlap is cropped from the underlying shape.

To combine shapes:

1   Select the shape that you want to combine with another shape. The shapes should not have a stroke color defined for them.

2   Move the selected shape over the other shape to place it in such a way that it represents the complex shape that you need.

3   Deselect the selected shape. The two shapes are combined as one shape.

After you combine the shapes, you cannot separate them.

Do it!

A-1: Combining shapes

Here's how	Here's why
1 Open Combining shapes	(From the current unit folder.) This file contains the various shapes that you'll use in the Web page.
Select the Oval Tool	
2 In the Toolbox, click as shown	To select the Stroke Color box.
Click ☑	(The No Color icon is in the Colors section of the Toolbox.) To specify that the oval will not have a stroke color.

3 In the Fill Color palette, type
#FF0000

Press (↵ ENTER)

4 Draw an oval as shown

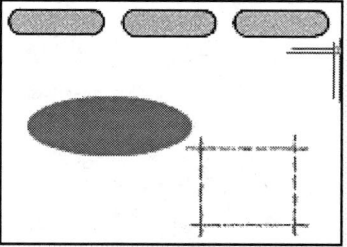

The oval is drawn without any outline.

Rotate the oval as shown

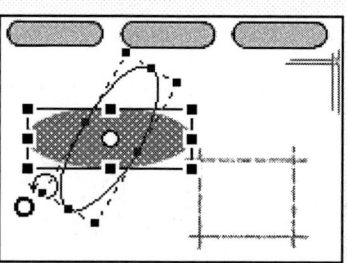

Use the Arrow Tool to select the shape, click the
Free Transform Tool and then click the Rotate
and Skew button in the Options section of the
Toolbox.

Deselect the Oval Tool

Select the Arrow Tool.

Move the oval as shown

Drag the oval near the lower edge of the Stage.

5 Create a copy of the oval   Choose Edit, Copy, and then choose Edit, Paste.

   Reduce the size of the copy of the
   oval as shown

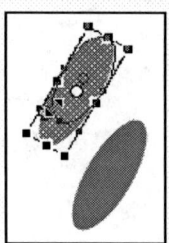

                                                     Click the Free Transform Tool and then use the
                                                     Scale button in the Options section of the
                                                     Toolbox.

   Rotate as shown

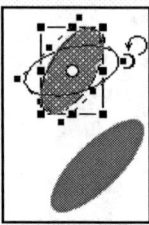

6 Drag the smaller oval as shown

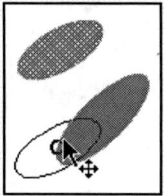

                                                     Use the Arrow Tool.

   Deselect the oval

   Click as shown

                                                     Both the ovals are selected indicating that they
                                                     are now combined.

   Deselect the combined shape

7 Change the stroke color to   Use the Stroke Color palette.
   #FF0000

   Change the fill color to #00CC00   Use the Fill Color palette.

   Draw an oval as shown

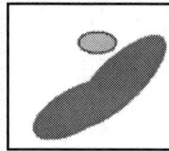

8 Double-click the new oval   Use the Arrow Tool.

   Rotate the oval as shown

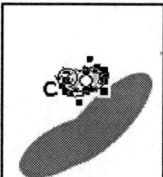

   Drag as shown

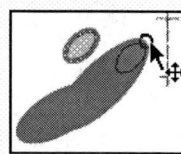

   Reduce the size of the oval as
   shown

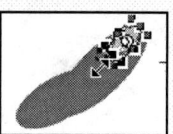

   Deselect the oval

9 Double-click as shown

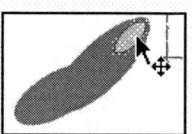

                                       To select the green oval.

10 Drag as shown

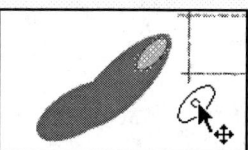

    Observe the shape   The area where the green oval overlapped the
                                       combined shape is cropped. This indicates that
                                       shapes with different fills do not combine.

11 Choose **Edit, Undo**   To place the green oval back on the combined
                                       shape.

    Deselect the shape

12 Save the file as
    My_combining_shapes

Grouping shapes

Explanation

You can group shapes to perform common actions on them, such as moving or applying color. To create a group, select the shapes that you want to include in the group and then choose Modify, Group. A blue rectangle appears around the shapes. This indicates that they are grouped. To ungroup shapes, select the group and choose Modify, Ungroup.

You can modify the group as well as the individual shapes in the group. To modify the group, double-click the group and make modifications. When you double-click the group, the images that are not included in the group appear faded. This indicates that the group is in the Edit mode. To deselect the group, double-click anywhere on the Stage. To modify an individual shape in the group, select the group and then select the shape and make the necessary modifications.

Do it!

A-2: Creating a group

Here's how	Here's why
1 Select all the rounded rectangles	Use marquee selection.
2 Choose **Modify**, **Group**	(To group the rectangles.) A blue rectangular outline appears around the selected rectangles indicating that they are grouped.
3 Double-click as shown	
	All the rounded rectangles are selected. Also, all the other shapes on the Stage appear faded. This is because the group is in the Edit mode.
Observe the upper left area of the screen	
	The name of the group (Group) appears indicating that the group is in the Edit mode.
4 Change the stroke color of the shapes in the selected group to #990099	Specify the color in the Stroke Color palette.
Deselect the rounded rectangles	The stroke color of all the rectangles in the group changes.

5 Select as shown

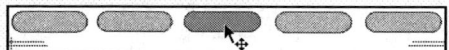

   Change the fill color of the
   selected rectangle to #CC66FF

   (Specify the color in the Fill Color palette.)
   Notice that the fill color of other rectangles in
   the group doesn't change.

   Deselect the rounded rectangle

   Double-click anywhere on the
   Stage

   (To deselect the group.) All the shapes are now
   clearly visible.

6 Click as shown

   To select the group.

7 Choose **Modify, Ungroup**

   To ungroup the rounded rectangles.

   Deselect the shapes

8 Update the file

Topic B: Using external images

Explanation

Flash gives you the option of importing images from other applications, such as Fireworks, Freehand, and Photoshop, and using file formats like EPS, GIF, JPEG, and BMP. These file types contain raster images, whereas in Flash, you create vector images, so to modify an imported raster image, you need to first convert it to a vector image.

Raster and vector graphics

There are two general types of graphic images: raster and vector. *Raster* graphics, such as bitmaps, are based on a grid of pixels. A *pixel* is the smallest whole unit of a graphic. This type of graphic is resolution dependent, which means that when you enlarge a raster image, the size of the pixel is increased, giving the picture a jagged look. Graphic packages, such as Adobe Photoshop, are used to create raster images.

Vector graphics are a series of points joined by lines. Vector images are resolution independent. This means that when you resize, rotate, magnify, or transform vector graphics, they do not loose their original clarity. These graphics need less storage space, are scalable, and are easier to port as compared to raster graphics. In Flash, you can create and edit vector graphics. Graphics packages such as Macromedia Freehand 9 and Adobe Illustrator are purely vector graphics software.

Importing images

To import a file:
  1   Choose File, Import. The Import dialog box appears.
  2   Verify that in the File of type list, All Formats is selected.
  3   Select the image you want to import and click Open. The file is imported in Flash.

When you import a raster image, the size of the Flash movie increases because raster images occupy more memory than vector images.

Do it!

B-1:   Importing graphics

Here's how	Here's why
1 Choose **File**, **Import...**	To open the Import dialog box.
2 Verify that in the Look in list, current unit folder is selected	
Verify that in the Files of type list, All Formats is selected	To view the files of all formats.
3 Select **Recipe**	This is a BMP file, which is a raster image.
4 Click **Open**	The file appears on the Stage.

5 Select the Free Transform Tool

   In the Options section, click the
   Scale modifier

   Resize as shown

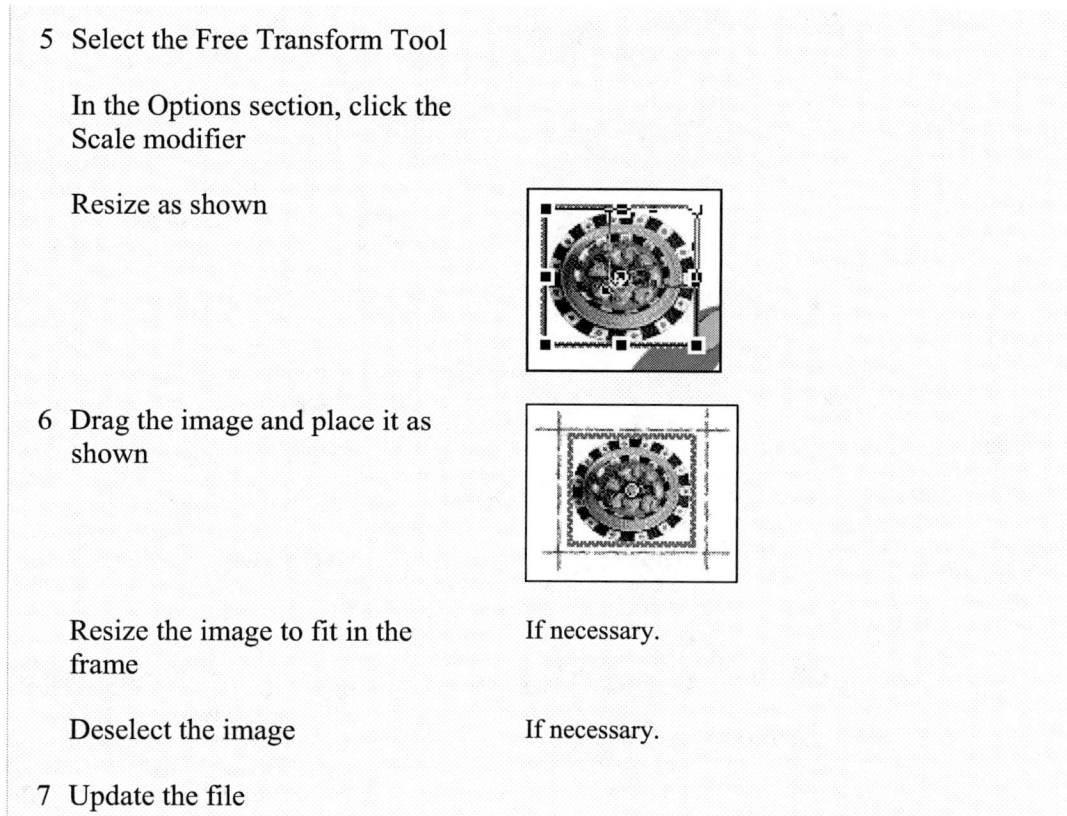

6 Drag the image and place it as
   shown

   Resize the image to fit in the   If necessary.
   frame

   Deselect the image   If necessary.

7 Update the file

Tracing bitmaps

Explanation   Flash will only recognize and edit vector images. So, you need to convert a raster image
               to a vector image before you can modify it, and you do that by tracing it.

               To trace an image:

               1 Select the imported image. A thatched border appears around the image.
               2 Choose Modify, Trace Bitmap. The Trace Bitmap dialog box appears, as shown
                  in Exhibit 4-1.
               3 Specify the settings for the various options in the dialog box and click OK.

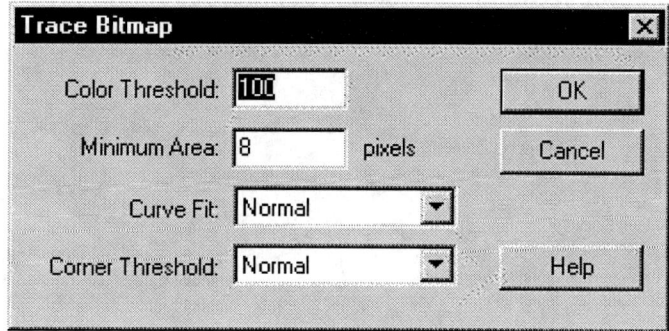

Exhibit 4-1: The Trace Bitmap dialog box

The following table describes the options in the Trace Bitmap dialog box:

Option	Description
Color Threshold	Minimum difference between the color values of two pixels so that they can be treated as different colors. This value determines the accuracy with which the colors are copied to the vector image. You can enter a value from 1 to 500 in this box.
Minimum Area	Number of pixels that are affected when you assign a color to a pixel. You use this value to specify the number of pixels that will have a consistent color when the raster image is converted to vector image. You can enter a value from 1 to 1000.
Curve Fit	The smoothness of the outlines of the image when converted to a vector image.
Corner Threshold	The sharpness that a shape will have.

Do it!

B-2: Converting raster images to vector images

Here's how	Here's why
1 Import Chili	(From the current unit folder.) Choose File, Import, select Chili and then, click Open.
Move the image	(To the left side of the Stage.)
Increase the size of the image	
Observe the image	The chili appears blurred.

2 Choose **Modify**, **Trace Bitmap...**	(To open the Trace Bitmap dialog box.) You'll convert this image to a vector image.
In the Color Threshold box, enter **50**	To specify the minimum difference between the color values of two pixels so that they can be treated as different colors.
In the Minimum Area box, enter **5**	To specify the number of pixels affected when you assign a color to a pixel.
3 From the Curve Fit list, select **Smooth**	To specify the smoothness of the vector image's outline.
From the Corner Threshold list, select **Many corners**	To specify the vector image's sharpness.
Click **OK**	The image appears with changes.
4 Deselect the image	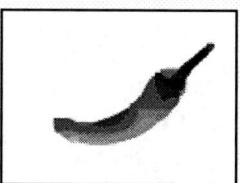
	The chili is no longer blurred and the corners are clearly visible. Also, the colors do not blend into each other.
5 Click as shown	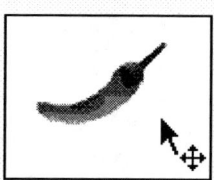
	The area around the shape is selected. This is the area that the imported shape occupies.
Press (DELETE)	To delete the selected area.
6 By using the Arrow Tool select as shown	
7 Change the fill color of the selected segment to #009900	
Deselect the selected area	To change the color of the selected segment to green.
8 Update and close the file	

Unit summary: Manipulating shapes and images

Topic A
In this unit, you learned how to **combine shapes** to create a new shape. You learned that you can only combine those shapes that have the same fill color and for which no stroke color is defined. You also learned how to **group shapes** to work with multiple shapes as a single unit.

Topic B
Finally, you learned how to **import raster images** and **convert raster images to vector images**. You learned that to modify an imported raster image, you first need to convert it to a vector image.

Independent practice activity

1 Open **Shapes practice**. (From the current unit folder.)

2 Group the two garlic shapes. (Hint: Select the shapes by using marquee selection.)

3 Change the stroke color of the shapes in the group to #CCCCCC.

4 Deselect the group.

5 Import **Spices**. (Hint: The file is in the current unit folder. If the **Resolve Library Conflict** dialogue box appears, verify that **Don't replace existing items** is selected and click **OK**.)

6 Resize and move the imported image, as shown in Exhibit 4-2.

7 Trace the image to have a value of **75** for Color Threshold, **12** for Minimum Area, **Very Tight** for Curve Fit, and **Few Corners** for Corner Threshold.

8 Save the file as **My_shapes_practice**.

9 Close the file.

Exhibit 4-2: The Stage after step 6 of the Independent Practice Activity

Unit 5

Inserting text

Unit time: 70 minutes

Complete this unit, and you'll know how to:

A Use the Text Tool to create an extending text block, a fixed text block, and a scrolling text block.

B Format text by changing the font, font size, font color, font style, and alignment.

Topic A: Using the Text Tool

Explanation   You can add text to a document by using the Text Tool in the Toolbox. The Text Tool creates a rectangle, called a *text block,* in which you type text. You can create three types of text blocks, extending, fixed, and scrollable. You can also convert one type of text block to another.

Adding fields

Fields are text blocks or text boxes that are contained within a form and are used to accept values from the user or to display labels. There are three types of field: static, dynamic, and input. *Static* text fields are used to display text, such as labels. You use *dynamic* text fields to display dynamically changing text, such as weather reports and stock quotes. *Input* text fields are used to get values from the user, such as username and password.

Extending text block

One type of text block that Flash employs is called the *extended text block*, which is used for short lines of text, such as titles or captions. You can identify an extending text block by a circle at its upper-right corner, as shown in Exhibit 5-1

To create an extending text block, you select the Text Tool, click on the Stage, and begin typing. It will expand horizontally as you continue to type text in it. If the text is too long to fit on the Stage, the text block extends into the work area. By default, the text appears in a single line on the Stage. To start a new line in the extending text block, press Enter.

Outlander Spices

Exhibit 5-1: An extending text block

To create an extending text block:
1   Select the Text Tool.
2   Click where you want to insert text.
3   Start typing the text. As you type, the text block expands to fit in the text.

Do it!

A-1: Creating an extending text block

Here's how	Here's why
1 Open Adding text	(From the current unit folder.) You'll add text to the Outlander Spices Web page.
2 Change the fill color to #000000	
3 Click [A]	(The Text Tool is in the Toolbox.) To select the Text Tool. The shape of the pointer changes to a plus sign with the letter A at its lower-right side.
4 Point as shown	
Click as shown	
	A rectangle with an insertion point inside it and a circle at its upper-right corner appears. Also, the shape of the pointer changes to a vertical "I" shaped beam.
5 Type **Welcome to Outlander Spices**	Notice that as you type the text, the text block extends to fit in the text.
Press (ESC)	To complete the text entry.
Deselect the text block	
6 Save the file as **My_adding_text**	

Fixed text block

Explanation

You use the *fixed text block* to add large blocks of text in a document. To add text to a fixed text block, first you need to create a frame. A *frame* is a boundary within which you want the text to appear. As you type the text, it wraps to the next line as it reaches the right edge of the frame.

Whereas the extending text block expands horizontally to accommodate the text, the fixed text block has a fixed width and expands downwards as lines wrap. To create a fixed text block, use the Text Tool and drag horizontally to the width of your choice. A square appears at the upper-right corner of the text block, as shown in Exhibit 5-2. You can resize a fixed text block by dragging this square.

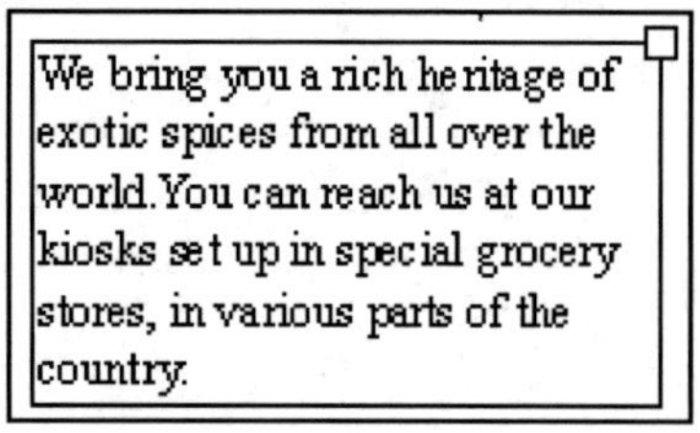

Exhibit 5-2: A fixed text block

To convert a fixed text block into an extending text block, double-click the square at its upper-right corner. To convert an extending text block to a fixed text block, drag the circle at its upper-right corner in any direction.

Do it!

A-2:   Creating a fixed text block

Here's how	Here's why
1 Verify that the Text Tool is selected	
2 Click as shown	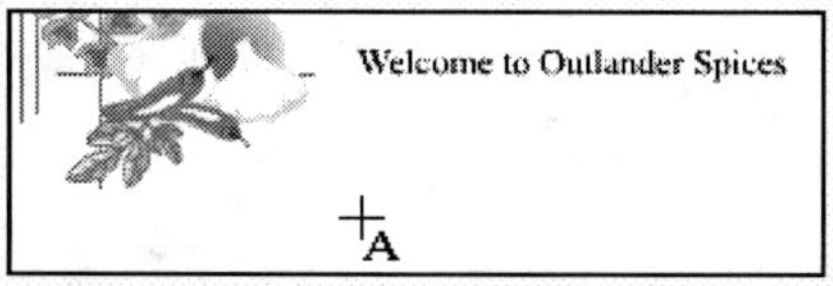
3 Drag as shown	
	When you release the mouse, a text block appears with an insertion pointer near its left edge and a square at its upper-right corner.
4 Type the text as shown	
	Notice that while typing, when you reach the right edge of the text block, the text automatically wraps to the next line.
Press (ESC)	
Deselect the text block	
5 Update the file	

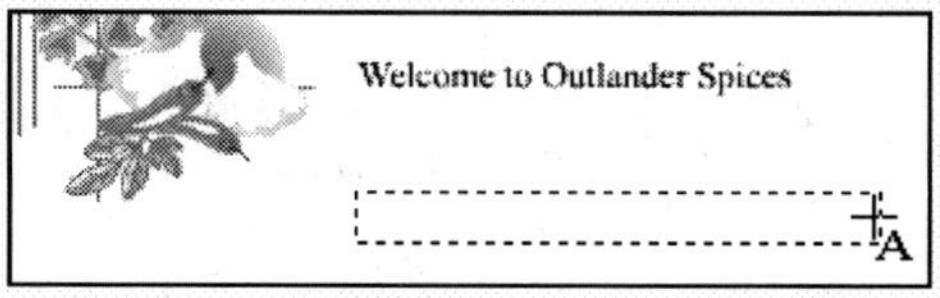

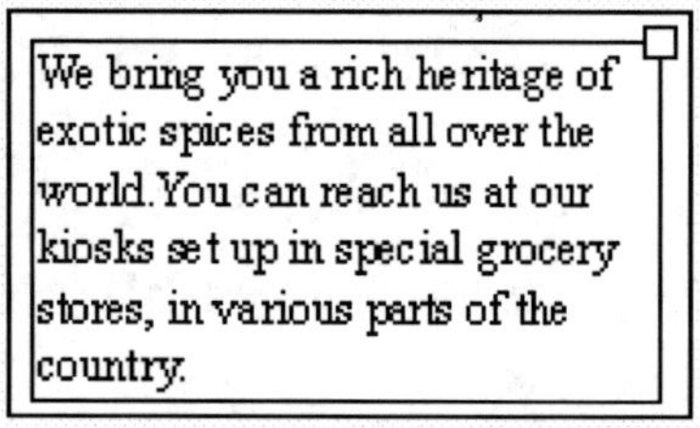

Scrollable text block

Explanation   Let's say you have a large block of text you need to fit in a small area but you still want it to be readable. One solution might be to use a *scrollable text block*. What you do is create a text block, add the text, and format it. Next, you resize the text block and move it to the correct location. Now, you attach a scroll bar to the text block so that more text will be displayed when the user scrolls down.

To create a scrollable text block:

1   Change the text type to Dynamic Text or Input Text, in the Properties panel.

2   From the Line type list, select Multiline.

3   Right-click the text block and choose Scrollable.

4   From the Components panel, drag and drop Scroll Bar.

```
We bring you a rich heritage of
exotic spices from all over the
world. You can reach us at our
kiosks set up in special grocery
stores, in various parts of the
country.
```

Exhibit 5-3: A scrollable text block

You can identify a scrollable text block by the solid black square that appears in the lower-right corner as shown in Exhibit 5-3.

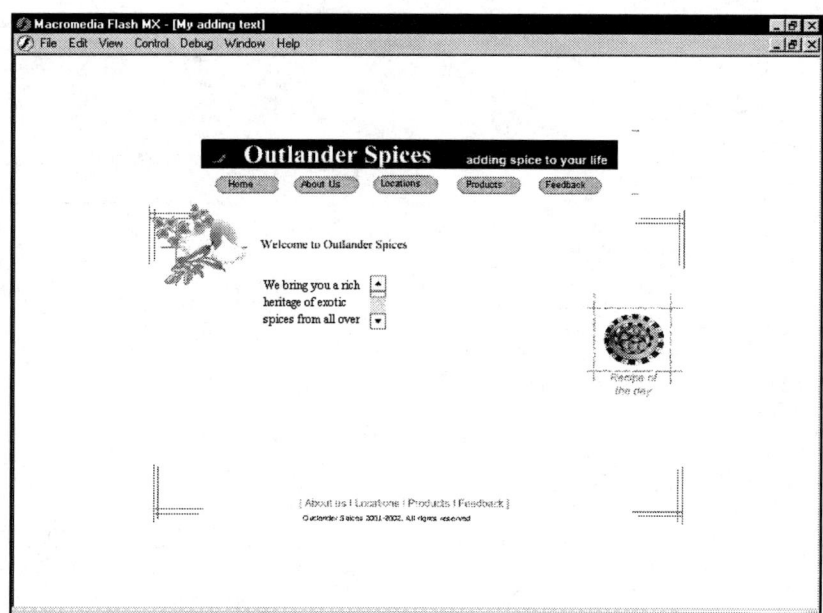

Exhibit 5-4: A sample movie window

You will not be able to scroll the text block in the Stage. To scroll the text you'll have to test the document. To test a document, choose Control, Test movie. The .fla file is converted into .swf format. A window, as shown in Exhibit 5-4 appears.

Do it!

A-3: Creating a scrollable text block

Here's how	Here's why
1 Select the text by using the Arrow Tool as shown	We bring you a rich heritage of exotic spices from all over the world. You can reach us at our kiosks set up in special grocery stores, in various parts of the country.
	A blue rectangle around the text block indicates that it is selected.
2 Open the Properties panel	Choose Window, Properties.
3 In the Properties panel, click as shown	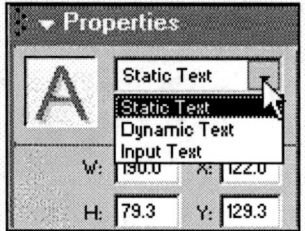
Select **Dynamic Text**	You'll convert the text from Static to Dynamic. Notice that Line type list and Instance Name is activated.
4 Click as shown	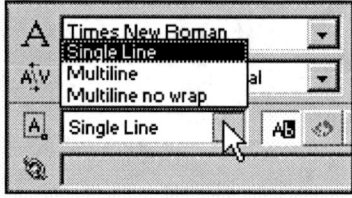
Select **Multiline**	To set the Line type as Multiline.
Close the Properties panel	
5 Right-click the text block	A shortcut menu appears.
From the shortcut menu, choose **Scrollable**	To convert the text block into a scrolling text block.
6 By using the Text Tool, click the text block	We bring you a rich heritage of exotic spices from all over the world. You can reach us at our kiosks set up in special grocery stores, in various parts of the country.
	A solid black square appears at the lower-right corner of the text block.

7 Drag as shown

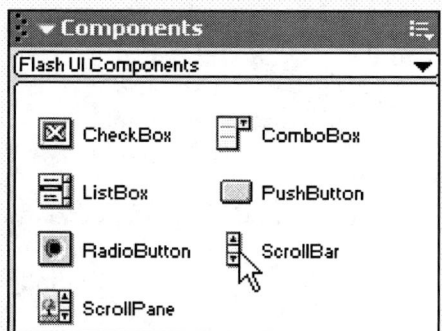

To reduce the size of the text block.

8 Choose **Window**, **Components**

To display the Components panel.

Maximize the Components panel

If necessary.

9 From the Components panel, drag the **ScrollBar**

Place the scrollbar as shown

By using the Free Transform Tool, resize the scroll bar as shown

10 Click the scroll bar and drag it
    into the text block, as shown

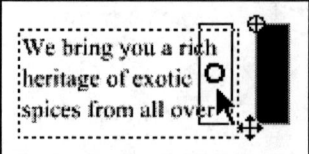

Use the Arrow Tool.

11 Choose **Control**, **Test Movie**

To convert it to the swf format. You'll be able to
scroll the text in this mode.

Click the scrollbar, as shown

Observe the text block

Notice that the text block scrolls.

Close the window

To return to the Edit mode.

Close the Components panel

12 Update the file

Topic B: Formatting text

Explanation You can change the text style, size, and color. You can position the text by setting margins and alignment for text blocks. You can also convert text characters to vector graphics to use them as shapes.

Selecting paragraphs

To format the text, first you need to select it. When you select the text, the text block is said to be in the Edit mode.

To select the text:

- Click the text to select the entire text block.
- Click and drag to select a specific part of the text in the text block.

Font and font size

You can change the font and font size of the text by using the Properties panel. *Font* is the design of the letters. *Font size* is the size of the characters. You change the font in the following two ways:

- In the Properties panel, from the Font list, select a font.
- Choose Text, Font, and choose an option from the submenu.

You change the font size in the following two ways:

- In the Properties panel, drag the font size slider until you get the value that you want for the font size.
- Choose Text, Size, and choose an option from the submenu.

Do it! ## B-1: Changing font and font size

Here's how	Here's why
1 Verify that the Arrow Tool is selected	
Click as shown	
	A blue rectangle around the text block indicates that it is selected.
2 Open the Properties panel	

3 In the Properties panel, click as shown

A list of the various fonts available in Flash appears.

From the list, select **Arial**

The font of the selected text changes to Arial.

4 Click as shown

A slider appears.

5 Drag the slider upwards until the value in the box is **30**

To change the font size of the selected text block to 30 pixels.

Click anywhere in the Properties panel

(If necessary.) To hide the slider.

Observe the text

Welcome to Outlander Spices

We bring you a rich heritage of exotic spices from all over

The selected text appears larger.

6 Click as shown

Welcome

We bring you a rich heritage of exotic spices from all over

Change the font size to 25

7 Update the file

Font style and color

Explanation   Font styles include Plain, Bold, Italic, Superscript, and Subscript. There are two ways to change the font style:

- In the Properties panel, click the Bold or the Italic button. For Superscript or Subscript, select from the Font position list.
- Choose Text, Style and choose an option from the submenu.

You apply color to text in the same way as you apply colors to shapes. To apply color to the text:

1 Select the text block.
2 In the Properties panel, click the color box to open the Text (fill) color palette and select a color.

Do it!   **B-2:   Changing font style and color**

Here's how	Here's why
1 Verify that the Arrow Tool is selected	
2 Click as shown	
	(Scroll up. If necessary.) To select the text block.
3 In the Properties panel, click **B**	To make the font bold.
4 Change the font style of About Us, Locations, Products, and Feedback to bold	Select the text and then click Bold in the Properties panel.
5 Point as shown	
Double-click the text	The text block is in the Edit mode.
Point as shown	
Select as shown	
	To select the text.
6 In the Properties panel, click as shown	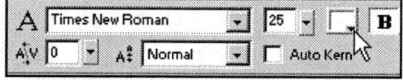
	To display the Text (fill) color palette.
In the Text (fill) color palette, click as shown	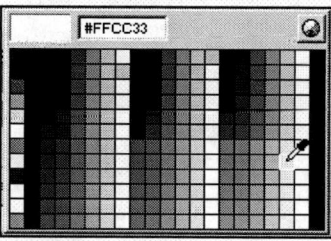
	(The hexadecimal value for this color is #FFCC33.) To change the color of the selected text to orange.

7 Select **Spices** as shown

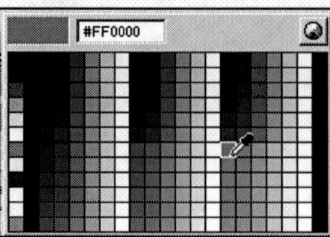

In the text color palette, click as shown

(The hexadecimal value for this color is #FF0000.) To change the color of the selected text to red.

8 Select the Arrow Tool

Click anywhere on the Stage | To deselect the text.

9 Update the file

Text alignment

Explanation

You can align text left or right, or center or justify. You can change alignments in the following two ways:

- Choose Text, Align, and choose an alignment option from the submenu.
- Select the text block, and in the Properties panel, click an alignment button.

Do it!

B-3: Aligning text

Here's how	Here's why
1 Verify that the Arrow Tool is selected	
2 Click as shown	Welcome to O We bring
	To select the text block.
3 In the Properties panel, click	The text is now centered.
4 Deselect the text block	
5 Update the file	

Skewing and scaling text

Explanation   You can change the size of the text block by using the Free Transform Tool. Here's how:

1   Select the text block.
2   Click the Free Transform Tool.
3   Use the Scale modifier.

You can also rotate and skew the text by using the Rotate and Skew modifier. With these options you can create mirror images of text.

Do it!   ### B-4:   Skewing and scaling a text block

Here's how	Here's why

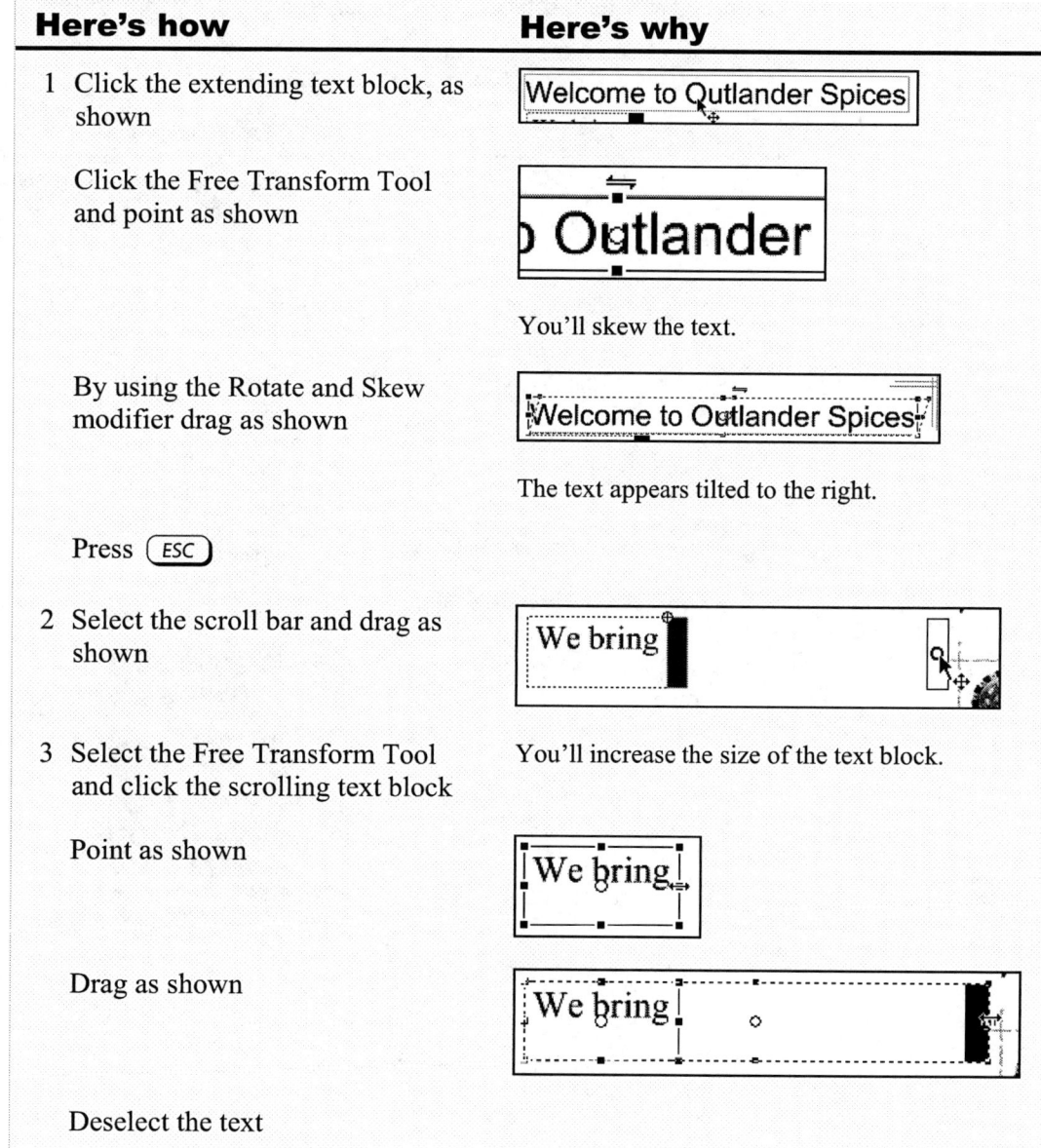

1   Click the extending text block, as shown

Click the Free Transform Tool and point as shown

You'll skew the text.

By using the Rotate and Skew modifier drag as shown

The text appears tilted to the right.

Press (ESC)

2   Select the scroll bar and drag as shown

3   Select the Free Transform Tool and click the scrolling text block

You'll increase the size of the text block.

Point as shown

Drag as shown

Deselect the text

4 Test the document	Choose Control, Test Movie.
Close the movie	
5 Update the file	

Breaking text apart

Explanation

You can manipulate individual characters of the text by converting them to vector shapes. To do so, you need to break apart the text.

To break apart text, select the text block and choose Modify, Break Apart.

Do it!

B-5:   Converting text to shapes

Here's how	Here's why
1 By using the Arrow Tool, point as shown	
Click the text block	To select the text block.
2 Choose **Modify, Break Apart**	You'll convert the text to a shape, and then modify it like a shape.
Press (ESC)	To deselect the shape.
3 Select the Zoom Tool	
Zoom on **Outlander Spices**	The text over the black rectangle.
4 Select the Arrow Tool and click as shown	
	A blue box appears around the letter.

5 Choose **Modify, Break Apart**   The blue box disappears.

   Click on the Stage   To deselect the letter.

   Point as shown

   The shape of the pointer changes.

   Drag as shown

   Observe the shape

   The shape is modified.

6 Modify as shown

   ![nde]

   Select the letter "d." Choose Modify, Break Apart, and drag the shape.

7 Switch to Show Frame view   The appearance of the letters is changed.

8 Update and close the file

Unit summary: Inserting text

Topic A   In this unit, you learned how to use the **Text Tool** to **create extending, fixed,** and **scrolling text block.**

Topic B   Finally, you learned how to **format text.** You changed the **font, font size, font style, font color,** and **text alignment.** You also learned how to **skew** and **scale** text blocks. You also **converted characters** to **vector shapes** to **modify** them.

Independent practice activity

1 Open **Text practice.**

2 Create a fixed text block and add the text **Outlander Spices** to it.

3 Create another fixed text block and add the text **adding spice to your life.**

4 Change the font size of "Outlander Spices" to **64.**

5 Change the font size of "adding spice to your life" to **28.**

6 Change the color of "Outlander Spices to" **#996600.**

7 Change the color of "adding spice to your life" to **#993333.**

8 Center the "Outlander Spices" text.

9 Close the Properties panel.

10 Resize and position the text blocks as shown in Exhibit 5-5.

11 Save the file as **My_text_practice.**

12 Close the file.

Exhibit 5-5: The Stage after step 10 of the Independent Practice Activity

Unit 6

Using layers

Unit time: 45 minutes

Complete this unit, and you'll know how to:

A Create, rearrange, and delete layers.

B Rename, lock, and hide layers.

Topic A: Introducing layers

Explanation

Layers are like transparent sheets of paper stacked on top of each other. Layers help you to organize and modify shapes. Just like a stack of paper, you can have different elements of an image on different layers. You can then combine these layers to form a composite image. For instance, if you have the image of an apple on one layer and a plate on another layer, you can stack the layers on top of each other to create an image of an apple on a plate. The advantage of using different layers is that you can edit specific areas of an image without affecting other shapes and images.

Layers list

You use the layers list in the Timeline, as shown in Exhibit 6-1, to create and name layers. You use the *Timeline* to arrange the shapes and images according to their sequence in the document. The layers list contains the names of all the layers in a document, from top to bottom. By default, when you create a new Flash document, it contains only one layer, named Layer 1.

You can make changes to only one layer at a time. The selected layer is highlighted in black in the layers list and a pencil icon appears next to the layer name, as shown in Exhibit 6-1.

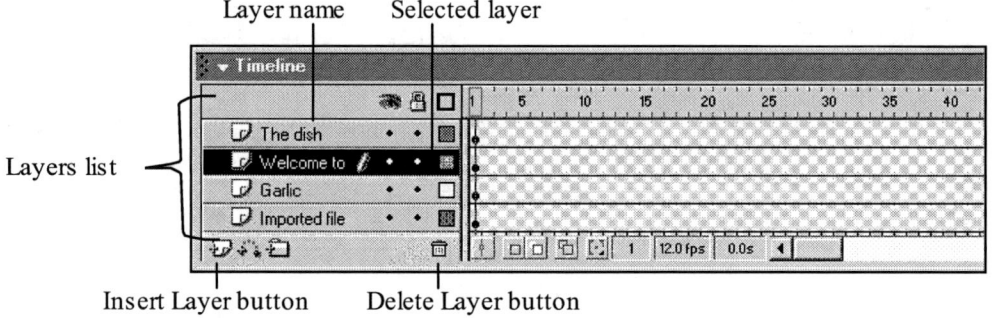

Exhibit 6-1: The layers list in the Timeline

Creating layers

You can create as many layers as you want. By default, the layers are named in the order in which they are created. For example, the first layer is named Layer 1 and second layer is named Layer 2. To create a layer, choose Insert, Layer. A new layer appears above the currently active layer. You can also create a new layer by clicking the Insert Layer button at the bottom of the layers list.

Do it!   **A-1:   Creating a layer**

Here's how	Here's why
1 Open Layers	(From the current unit folder.) This file contains the shapes and images of the Outlander Spices Home page arranged in layers. You'll create a new layer in this file.
2 Verify that the Arrow Tool is selected	
3 Click 🔲	The Insert Layer button is at the bottom of the layers list. You'll create a new layer and add a shape to it.
Observe the layers list	A new layer, Layer 8, is added in the layers list and is selected.
4 Select as shown	
Observe the layers list	Garlic layer is now selected indicating that this is the active layer and the selected chilies are in this layer.
5 Choose **Edit, Cut**	The chilies disappear from the garlic layer.
6 From the layers list, select **Layer 8**	You'll add the chilies to this layer.
7 Choose **Edit, Paste in Place**	(To add the chilies to this layer.) The chilies reappear on the Stage behind the other shapes. Notice that in the layers list, Layer 8 is selected. This indicates that now the chilies are in this layer.
Deselect the chilies	
8 Save the file as **My_layers**	

Rearranging layers

Explanation

By default, the top-most layer in the layers list appears on the top of the Stage with all other layers appearing beneath it. You can change order of the layers, and this will affect the position of each layer and the objects and images on them. You can also merge any number of layers into a single layer.

Changing the order of layers

To change the position of a layer, select it in the layers list, and drag it above the layer over which you want to place it.

Merging layers

You can merge layers when you want all the components on those layers to act as a composite image. You can merge as many layers as you want. To merge layers:

1 Select the layers whose contents you want to merge. The contents of the selected layers appear selected on the Stage.
2 Choose Edit, Cut. The contents of the selected layers disappear from the Stage.
3 Select the layer in which you want to place the contents.
4 Choose Edit, Paste in Place. The contents of the layers merge and reappear on the Stage.

Do it!

A-2: Merging and rearranging layers

Here's how	Here's why
1 Verify that the Arrow Tool is selected	
2 From the layers list, select as shown	

	This is the Imported back layer. You'll merge this layer with another layer.
3 Remove the contents of this layer	Choose Edit, Cut.
4 From the layers list, select **The dish**	You'll create a new layer above this layer.
Create a new layer	(Click the Insert layer button.) Notice that Layer 9 appears above The Dish layer.

5 Add the contents of the Imported back layer to layer 9	(Choose Edit, Paste in Place.) The contents of the two layers are now merged.
Observe the Stage	Only the background of the Web page is now visible. This indicates that layer 9 is the topmost layer now.
6 Verify that layer 9 is selected	
7 Drag layer 9 as shown	

As you drag, a thatched line appears.

Release the left mouse button when the line is below the Imported back layer	The images that were not visible earlier are now visible.
8 Drag layer 8 and place it above the garlic layer	To view the chilies clearly.
9 Update the file	

Deleting layers

Explanation

When you delete a layer, it's content is removed from the Stage. To delete a layer, click the Delete Layer button or drag the layer to the Delete Layer button at the bottom of the layers list. You can also right-click the layer and choose Delete Layer.

Do it!

A-3: Deleting a layer

Here's how	Here's why
1 Select the **Imported back** layer	You'll delete this layer, because it's content is merged with layer 9.
2 Click 🗑	The Delete Layer button is at the bottom of the layers list.
Observe the layers list	The Imported back layer no longer appears in the list.
3 Update the file	

Topic B: Modifying layers

Explanation

Default layer names like Layer 3 aren't very descriptive. You can change the layer's name to something more meaningful. To prevent a layer from being modified, you can either lock that specific layer so it can't be edited, or hide it so that it's not visible.

Renaming layers

You rename in one of these two ways:

- Choose Modify, Layer to open the Layer Properties dialog box, and in the Name box, specify the name. You can also right-click a layer and choose Properties to open the Layer Properties dialog box.
- Double-click the layer, type the new name for the layer, and press Enter.

Do it!

B-1: Renaming a layer

Here's how	Here's why
1 Select Layer 8	You'll change this layer's name.
2 Choose **Modify, Layer...**	To open the Layer Properties dialog box.
3 Edit the Name box to read **Chilies**	To specify a name for the layer.
Click **OK**	
4 Double-click the Welcome to layer	The layer name is selected with the insertion point appearing at the end of the selection.
Edit the text to read **All text**	To specify a new name for the layer.
Press (↵ ENTER)	
5 Update the file	

Locking layers

Explanation

Locking layers prevents you from making changes in the contents of the layers. When you lock a layer, a lock icon appears in the Lock column of the layers list, as shown in Exhibit 6-2. After locking a layer, if you select any of the Line, Oval, Rectangle, or Pencil tools and move the pointer on the Stage, the pointer changes to a pencil with a circle having a line across it. This indicates that the layer is locked.

Lock/Unlock All Layers button

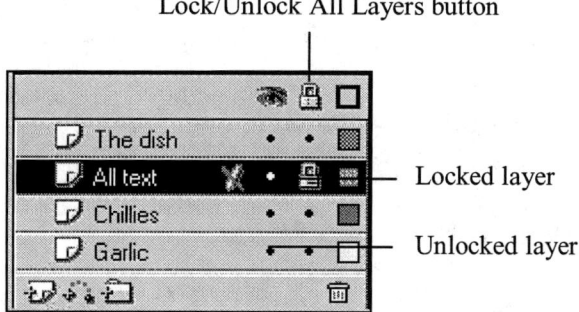

Locked layer

Unlocked layer

Exhibit 6-2: A locked and unlocked layer

To lock a layer, you can either:

- Click the dot in the Lock column next to the layer name in the layers list.
- Open the Layer Properties dialog box and check the Lock option for that layer.

To unlock a layer, you can either:

- Click the lock icon in the Lock column next to the layer name in the layers list.
- Open the Layer Properties dialog box and clear the Lock option for that layer.

To lock all the layers except the selected layer, right-click the selected layer and choose Lock Others. To unlock these layers, right-click the selected layer and choose Show All. To lock all the layers in a document, click the Lock/Unlock All Layers button, shown in Exhibit 6-2.

Hiding layers

Hiding a layer hides it's content from the Stage. You cannot edit or print the content of a hidden layer. You hide a layer when you want to modify a layer below it. To hide a layer, you can either:

- Click the dot in the Eye column next to the layer name in the layers list.
- Open the Layer Properties dialog box and clear the Show option for that layer.

An "X" appears in the Eye column for a hidden layer, as shown in Exhibit 6-3, and the content of that layer disappears from the Stage.

Visible layer

Show/Hide All
Layers button

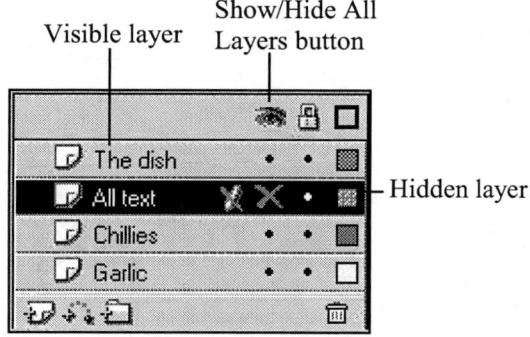

Hidden layer

Exhibit 6-3: A hidden and visible layer

To show a hidden layer, you can either:
- Click the cross icon in the Eye column next to the layer name in the layers list.
- Open the Layer Properties dialog box and check the Show option for that layer.

To hide all the layers except the selected layer, right-click the selected layer and choose Hide Others. To unlock these layers, right-click the selected layer and choose Show All. To hide all the layers in a document, click the Show/Hide All Layers button.

Do it!

B-2:   Locking and hiding a layer

Here's how	Here's why
1 In the layers list, verify that All text is selected	You'll lock this layer.
2 Open the Layer Properties dialog box	Choose Modify, Layer.
3 Check **Lock**	To lock the layer.
Click **OK**	
	Notice that in the layers list, a lock appears in the Lock column for the All text layer. This indicates that this layer is locked. Also, notice that the pencil icon has a red line through it. This indicates that you cannot modify this layer.
4 Select the Text Tool	You'll try to edit the locked layer.
Click the Stage	A message box appears warning you that the layer is either locked or hidden.
Click **No**	
5 Select the Arrow Tool	
Select the Garlic layer	
Open the Layer Properties dialog box	

6	Clear **Show**	To hide the layer.
	Click **OK**	The shapes near the top left edge of the Stage are no longer visible.
	Observe the Garlic layer	

Notice that the dot in the Eye column changes to a cross. This indicates that the layer is no longer visible. Also, notice that the pencil icon has a red line through it. This indicates that you cannot modify the layer.

7	Click as shown	

(To unhide the layer.) The shapes contained in the layer appear on the Stage.

8	Right-click The dish layer	You'll hide all layers to display the dish.
	Choose **Hide Others**	To hide the contents of all the layers other than The dish layer.
9	Right-click The dish layer	You'll unhide all layers.
	Choose **Show All**	The contents of all the layers are again visible on the Stage.
10	Update and close the file	

Unit summary: Using layers

Topic A   In this unit, you learned how to work with **layers**. You learned that to **create** a layer you can use the **Insert Layer button**, to **rearrange** layers you can drag layers and arrange them, and to **delete layers** you can use the **Delete Layer button**.

Topic B   Finally, you learned how to **modify layers**. You learned that to **rename** a layer you can use the **Layer Properties dialog box**, to **lock** a layer you can click the **Lock/Unlock All Layers button**, and to **hide a layer** you can click the **Show/Hide All Layers button**.

Independent practice activity

1 Open **Layers practice**.

2 Create a new layer and move all the text to this layer. (Hint: The text is currently assigned to the Shapes layer.)

3 Rename the new layer as **Text**.

4 Place the Shapes layer at the bottom of the layers list.

5 Lock the Spices layer.

6 Hide the Lines layer.

7 Save the file as **My_layers_practice**.

8 Close the file.

Unit 7

Introducing animation and templates

Unit time: 45 minutes

Complete this unit, and you'll know how to:

A Use the Timeline and frames in an animation.

B Create a frame-by-frame animation and use Onion Skin to modify the contents of various frames.

C Work with templates.

Topic A: Animation basics

Explanation

An *animation* is a series of related shapes and images that create an illusion of motion when they are shown in sequence. You can create an animation by creating a shape or text that moves on the stage, or by making a shape or text change its parameters, such as color or size.

You can create two types of animations in Flash, frame-by-frame and tweened. When you create a *frame-by-frame* animation, you have to create the different variations of the shapes manually. However, in *tweened* animation, you only need to create the shapes for the start and end of the animation. Flash automatically creates the intermediate shapes.

Frames and Timeline

To create an animation in Flash, it is important to know about frames and Timeline. A *frame* is a placeholder where you place the the images needed for the animation from the start to the end. You insert keyframes between frames in an animation. A *keyframe* is a frame in which you change the appearance of an image in the animation.

The order in which the frames are arranged and shown is important for effective animation. The Timeline helps you arrange the frames. The Timeline is divided into two sections, as shown in Exhibit 7-1. The section on the left contains the layers list for a document, and the one on the right contains the Timeline, the frames, and the playhead.

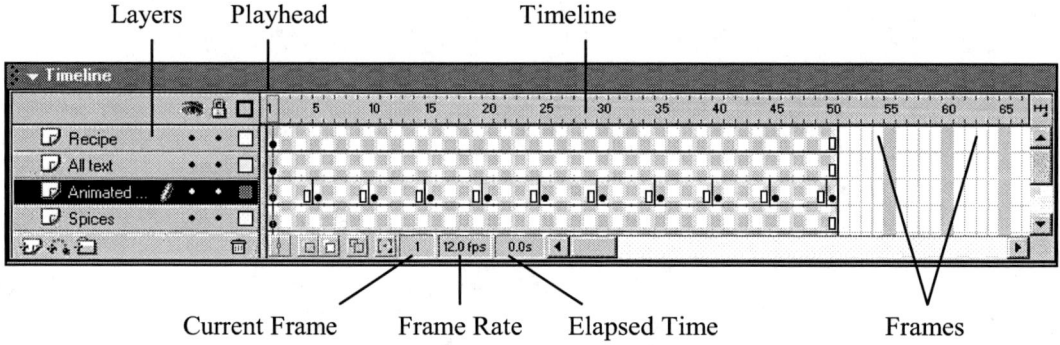

Exhibit 7-1: The Timeline

The following table describes the various components of the Timeline:

Item	Description
Playhead	As you move the playhead in the Timeline, the content of the frame below it appears on the Stage.
Current Frame	Displays the frame number over which the playhead is currently placed.
Frame Rate	Displays the number of frames over which the playhead moves in one second.By default, the playhead moves over the Timeline in such a way that it covers 12 frames in one second. You can change the Frame Rate by double-clicking the Frame Rate box. The Document Properties dialog box appears in which you can change the Frame Rate box.
Elapsed Time	Displays the time that the playhead takes in moving over all the frames in the animation. The value in the Elapsed Time box is related to the value in the Frame Rate box. If the Frame Rate is more, the Elapsed Time is less and if the Frame Rate is less, the Elapsed time is more.

Do it!

A-1: Understanding animations

Here's how	Here's why
1 Open Animation	(From the current unit folder.) This file contains Outlander Spices Home page.
Switch to Show Frame view	
2 Choose **Control**, **Play**	To play the document.
Observe the Stage	Notice the moving chili and the changing gradient of the circle.
Observe the Timeline	The document progresses as the playhead moves across the Timeline, and the values in the Current Frame and the Frame Rate boxes change accordingly.
3 Press (ESC)	To stop the animation.
4 Close the file	A warning message appears prompting you to save the changes.
Click **No**	To close the file without saving the changes.

Topic B: Creating animations

Explanation

The first step in creating a frame-by-frame animation is to create the image with which you want to start the animation. To complete the animation, you add the modified versions of the image to the keyframes that you insert in the Timeline.

You can modify the various stages of an animation. You can view the components of all the keyframes and then modify them separately.

Creating basic animations

To create a frame-by-frame animation:

1   Create an image. By default, this image is automatically placed in the keyframe that is present in the Timeline.
2   In the Timeline, click the frame where you want to insert the keyframe.
3   Choose Insert, Keyframe to insert the keyframe. You can also press F6 or right-click and select Insert Keyframe.
4   Modify the image in the keyframe.
5   Repeat steps two through four to add more keyframes.

Do it!

B-1:   Creating a frame-by-frame animation

Here's how	Here's why
1 Open Basic animation	(From the current unit folder.) You'll create an animation that is an illusion of a chili moving across the Stage.
Switch to Show Frame view	
2 Verify that the Arrow Tool is selected	
Select the **Animated chili** layer	You'll add animation in this layer.
3 In the Timeline, point as shown	
	You'll insert a keyframe in this frame.
Click the Frame	The playhead is now over the frame. Also, the color of the frame changes to blue indicating that the frame is selected.

4 Choose **Insert**, **Keyframe**

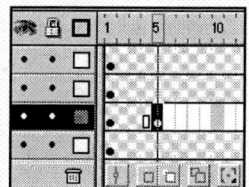

A white dot appears in the frame indicating that a keyframe is inserted. Also, the color of the frames from frame 1 to frame 5 changes to gray. This indicates that the appearance of the shape will remain the same in these frames.

5 Move the chili as shown

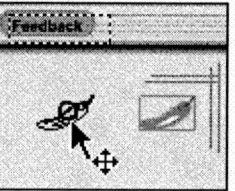

To specify the next position of the chili for the animation.

6 Click as shown

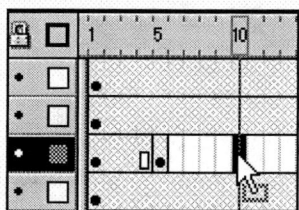

This is frame 10.

Insert a keyframe in this frame   Choose Insert, Keyframe.

Move the chili as shown

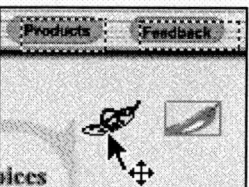

7 Insert a keyframe in frame 15

Change the position of the chili as shown

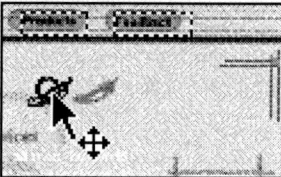

8 Insert a keyframe in frame 20,25,30,35,40,45,and 50, and at each keyframe, move the chili to the left	Move the chili slightly towards the left edge for each keyframe.
9 Play the document	(Choose Control, Play.) The chili moves from right to left creating an illusion of motion.
10 Save the file as **My_basic_animation**	

Onion Skins

If you are not playing an animation, the contents of the currently selected frame appear on the Stage. By default, the contents of the first frame appear on the Stage. However, you can view the contents of all the keyframes by using Onion Skin. To use Onion Skin, click the Onion Skin button at the bottom of the Timeline, as shown in Exhibit 7-2. Onion skin markers appear on the Timeline scale. You can drag these to display the content of all the keyframes on the Stage. You can modify all the keyframes at the same time with the help of the Edit Multiple Frames button in the Timeline.

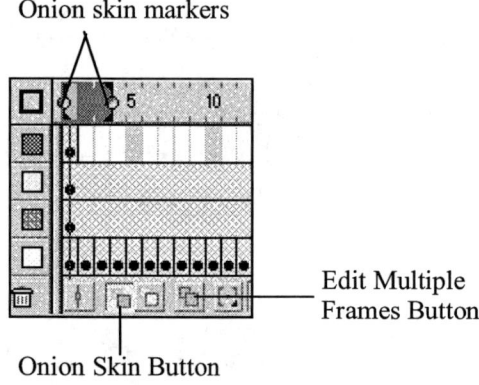

Exhibit 7-2: A part of the Timeline

Exhibit 7-3: The positions of the chili in the various keyframes after rotating them

Do it!   **B-2:   Using Onion Skin**

Here's how	Here's why
1 Verify that the Animated chili layer is selected	You'll modify the keyframes of the animation created in this layer to add the effect of a rotating chili.
Click frame 1	In the Timeline.
2 Click	(The Onion Skin button is at the bottom of the Timeline.) To view the various keyframes created in a layer.
Observe the Timeline	
	Onion Skin markers appear on the Timeline scale. The left marker over frame 1 has a dark pink color, indicating that the Onion Skin starts from this frame. The right marker that is colored black indicates where the Onion Skin ends.
3 Point as shown	
Drag as shown	
	Drag the right marker to frame 50.
Observe the Stage	The position of the chili in the various keyframes appears on the Stage. However, these images are dim.

4 Click 🔲	(The Edit Multiple Frames button is at the bottom of the Timeline.) You'll modify the contents of multiple frames at the same time.
Observe the Stage	The chili in all the keyframes is now clearly visible.
Rotate the chili as shown	
5 Click the keyframe in frame 5 of the Animated chili layer	The chili corresponding to this keyframe is selected.
Rotate the chili as shown	
6 Click frame 15	
Rotate the selected chili as shown	
7 Rotate the chili in frame 20 as shown	
8 Rotate the chili in the remaining keyframes	As shown in Exhibit 7-3.
9 Click 🔲	(The Edit Multiple Frames button.) To deselect the chili in the various keyframes.
Click 🔲	(The Onion Skin button.) To hide the contents of the keyframes.
10 Play the document	The chili now moves across the Stage creating an illusion of rotation. Note that the chili moves across the Stage only once.
11 Choose **Control**, **Loop Playback**	To continuously play the document.
Play the document	The chili moves from one end of the Stage to the other in a continuous loop.
Press (ESC)	
12 Update the file	

Topic C: Working with templates

Explanation

Templates are the basic structure of a document. You can create templates in Flash to save time and effort. You can either customize the existing templates or create your own templates. Flash provides templates for Ads, Quiz, Broadcast, Mobile Devices, Menus, Photo Slide Show, and Presentation. To create your on templates, you can save an existing document as a template.

Saving documents as templates

A document can be saved as a template to use the same properties for various documents. The various properties are background, frame size, animation, images, codes, and text fields.

To save a document as template:

1   Choose File, Save as Template.
2   In the Save As Template dialog box, enter the Name, Category, and Description of the template.
3   Click Save.

Do it!

C-1:   Saving a document as a template

Here's how	Here's why
1 Choose **File, Save As Template...**	The Save As Template dialog box appears.
2 In the Name box, type **Outlander_Spices**	To specify the name of the Template.
3 In the Category list, type **Website**	To specify the name of Category.
4 In the Description box, type **Use this template to create a Web page with animation**	To provide a description for the template.
5 Click **Save**	To save the template.
6 Close the file	

Creating new documents by using templates

Explanation

You can use templates to create photo galleries, banner ads, custom presentations, or an online quiz. You can use the PhotoSlideshow template in Flash to create a slide show of photos. The Menu template can be used to create menus. You can use the Presentation template to present annual reports of an organization.

To create a new document:

1 Choose File, New From Template.
2 In the New Document dialog box, select the category and category item.
3 Click Create.

Do it!

C-2: Creating a new document by using templates

Here's how	Here's why
1 Choose **File, New From Template...**	A New Document dialog box appears. You'll create a new document by using Templates.
2 Under Category, click **Ads**	Notice that in the Preview box a template appears.
3 Under Category Items list, verify that banner_468x60 is selected	You'll create an advertisement banner for Outlander Spices.
4 Click **Create**	A guide about guidelines for ad format appears.
5 Verify that _instructions layer is selected	You'll delete this layer.
Delete the _instructions layer	(Click the Delete Layer button at the bottom of the layers list.) The template for banner ad is now visible.
6 Import Recipe	(From the current unit folder.) Choose File, Import, select Recipe and then, click Open.
Resize the image to fit in the Stage	Use the Free Transform Tool.
Using the Arrow Tool, move the image to the left, as shown	

7 Import Spices

(From the current unit folder.) Choose File, Import, select Spices and then, click Open.

Resize the image to fit in the Stage

Move the image to the right, as shown

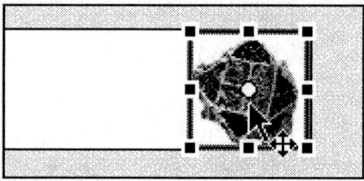

8 Insert a keyframe in frame 10

Right-click the frame and choose Insert Keyframe.

9 Select the Text Tool and click as shown

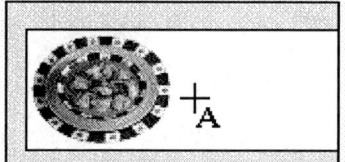

Enter **Outlander Spices**

Change the font to **Arial**

Change the font size to **40**

Move the text block, as shown

10 Insert a keyframe in frame 20

11 Import Chili

(From the current unit folder.) Choose File, Import, select Chili and then, click Open.

Resize the image

Place the image as shown

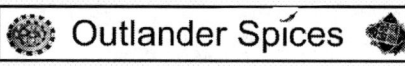

12 Play the document

13 Save the file as **My_banner**

Close the file

Unit summary: Introducing animation and templates

Topic A   In this unit, you learned **animation basics**. You learned that an animation is a series of related shapes and images that create an illusion of motion when they are shown in sequence. You also learned that to **play an animation** you choose **Control, Play**.

Topic B   Next, you learned how to create a **frame-by-frame animation**. You also learned that to view the components of multiple keyframes you can **use Onion Skin** and to modify the components of various frames you can use the **Edit Multiple Frames** button.

Topic C   Finally, you learned how to **save a document as a template** and **create a new document from a template**.

Independent practice activity

1 Open **Animation practice**.

2 In the Text layer, insert keyframes at frames 5, 10, 15, 20, 25, and 30.

3 Open the Color Mixer panel. (Hint: Choose Window, Color Mixer.)

4 Verify that the Text layer is selected.

5 In the Mixer panel, change the value of Alpha for keyframes 5 and 25 to **75%**.

6 Change the value of Alpha for keyframes 10 and 20 to **50%**.

7 Change the value of Alpha for keyframe 15 to **25%**.

8 Play the animation.

9 Save the file as a template. In the Name box, enter **My_Outlander_Spices**. From the Category list, select **Website.**

10 Close the file.

11 Close Flash.

Flash MX: Basic

Course summary

This summary contains information to help you bring the course to a successful conclusion. Using this information, you will be able to:

A Use the summary text to reinforce what you've learned in class.

B Determine the next courses in this series (if any), as well as any other resources that might help you continue to learn about Flash MX.

Topic A: Course summary

Use the following summary text to reinforce what you've learned in class.

Flash MX: Basic

Unit 1

In this unit, you learned how to **start Flash** and **open a file**. You examined the various **components of the Flash window**, including **panels** and **Toolbox**. Next, you learned how to use the **Flash Help** feature including the **Contents tab**, **Index tab**, and **Search tab**. Finally, you learned how to **close** a file and **exit** Flash.

Unit 2

In this unit, you learned how to **create basic shapes** by using drawing tools such as **Line Tool**, the **Rectangle Tool** and the **Oval Tool**. You also learned how to create freeform shapes and curves by using the **Pencil Tool** and the **Pen Tool**. Then you learned how to use the **Arrow Tool** for marquee selection, the **Subselection Tool** to select anchor points, the **Lasso Tool** to select irregular shapes, and the **Free Transform Tool** to modify shapes. Next you learned how to magnify images by using the **Zoom Tool** and the **Hand Tool**. You also learned how to use the **Eraser Tool**. Finally, you learned how to **handle shapes**. You also learned how to **Copy**, **Move**, and **Delete** Shapes.

Unit 3

In this unit, you learned how to use the **Fill Color** box and the **Stroke Color** box. You also learned how to apply **fill color** and **stroke color** to a shape by using the **Paint Bucket Tool** and the **Ink Bottle Tool**, respectively. Then you learned how to use the **Eyedropper Tool** to **copy** the **fill** and **stroke color** of one shape to another. Next, you learned how to use the **Brush Tool** to add brush-like strokes to shapes. Finally, you learned how to **create** and **save custom colors**, **swatches**, and **line styles** by using the **Color Mixer panel**, the **Properties panel**, and the **Stroke Style dialog box**.

Unit 4

In this unit, you learned how to **combine shapes** to create a new shape. You also learned how to **group** shapes to work with multiple shapes as a single unit. Finally, you learned how to import raster images and convert **raster images to vector images**.

Unit 5

In this unit, you learned how to use the **Text Tool** to create **extending**, **fixed**, and **scrolling text block**. Next, you learned how to **format text**. You changed the **font, font size, font style, font color**, and **text alignment**. Then, you learned how to **skew** and **scale** text blocks. Finally, you learned how to **convert characters** to **vector shapes** to **modify** them.

Unit 6

In this unit, you learned how to work with **layers**. You also learned how to **create, rearrange**, and **delete layers**. Then, you learned how to **modify layers**. Finally, you learned how to **rename, lock**, and **hide** a **layer**.

Unit 7

In this unit, you learned **animation basics**. You also learned how to **play an animation**. Then, you learned how to create a **frame-by-frame animation**. You also learned how to use **Onion Skin** to view the components of multiple keyframes. Next, you used the **Edit Multiple Frames** button to modify the components of various frames. Finally, you learned how to **save a document as a template** and **create a new document from a template**.

Topic B: Continued learning after class

It is impossible to learn to use any software effectively in a single day. To get the most out of this class, you should begin working with Flash MX to perform real tasks as soon as possible. Course Technology also offers resources for continued learning.

Next courses in this series

This is the first course in this series. The next course in this series is:

- *Flash MX: Advanced*

Other resources

You might find some of these other Course Technology resources useful as you continue to learn about Flash MX. For more information, visit www.course.com.

- *Multimedia Projects for Macromedia Flash MX and Dreamweaver MX*
  ISBN: 0-619-05514-6

Flash MX: Basic

Quick reference

Button	Shortcut keys	Function
	N	Creates line segments
	R	Creates rectangles and squares
	O	Creates ovals and circles
	P	Creates curves
	Y	Creates freeform shapes
		Draws straight lines when used with the Pencil Tool
		Smoothes out any sharp areas in a selected shape
		Straightens out any curves in a selected shape
		Helps to distort a selected shape
		Helps warp and distort objects
	V	Selects and modifies shapes
	A	Selects the anchor points in a shape and modifies them
	L	Makes irregular selections

Button	Shortcut keys	Function
	H	Displays documents in the Show Frame view
	Z	Displays documents in a magnified form
	Q	Transforms objects, groups, instances, or text blocks
		Rotates shapes
		Resizes shapes
	E	Removes parts of a shape
		Erases only the fills of a selected shape
	K	Changes the fill color of the selected shapes
	S	Changes the stroke color of the selected shapes
	I	Copies the fill color or the stroke color of one shape to another
	B	Adds brush like strokes in a document
		Applies brush strokes over any strokes or fills over which you move the pointer
		Creates a shape with no fill or stroke color
	T	Adds text to a document
		Makes the selected text bold
		Center aligns the selected text
		Creates a new layer
		Deletes the selected layer
		Makes the components of multiple frames visible
		Edits the components of multiple frames

Index

V

Z